BEYOND THE VEIL

Fatima Mernissi

Saqi Books

Beyond the Veil

Male–Female Dynamics
in Modern Muslim Society

British Library Cataloguing-in-Publication Data
A catalogue record for this book is available from the
British Library

ISBN 0 86356 441 0

First published 1975 by
Schenkman Publishing Company, Inc.
Cambridge, Massachusetts
© Fatima Mernissi 1975

Additional material Editions Tierce
© Editions Tierce 1983

The revised edition first published 1985 by Saqi Books
© Saqi Books for the revised edition

This edition published 2003

Saqi Books
26 Westbourne Grove
London W2 5RH

www.saqibooks.com

Contents

Preface: A Note to the Western Reader   7
Introduction: Roots of the Modern Situation   11

Part One   The Traditional Muslim View of Women and   25
Their Place in the Social Order

1. The Muslim Concept of Active Female Sexuality   27
2. Regulation of Female Sexuality in the Muslim   46
       Social Order
3. Sex and Marriage Before Islam   65

Part Two   Anomic Effects of Modernization on   87
Male–Female Dynamics

4. The Modern Situation: Moroccan Data   89
5. Sexual Anomie As Revealed by the Data   97
6. Husband and Wife   108
7. The Mother-in-Law   121
8. The Meaning of Spatial Boundaries   137
9. The Economic Basis of Sexual Anomie in Morocco   148

Conclusion: Women's Liberation in Muslim Countries   165

Notes   179
Index   195

Preface
A Note to the
Western Reader

Is there a nascent female liberation movement in the Middle East and North Africa similar to those appearing in Western countries? For decades this kind of question has blocked and distorted analysis of the situation of Muslim women, keeping it at the level of senseless comparisons and unfounded conclusions. It is a well-established tradition to discuss Muslim women by comparing them, implicitly or explicitly, to Western women. This tradition reflects the general pattern that prevails in both East and West when the issue is 'who is more civilized than whom'.

When the Muslim countries were defeated and occupied by the West, the colonizers used all available means to persuade the defeated Muslims of their inferiority in order to justify foreign occupation. Muslims were dismissed as promiscuous, and many crocodile tears were shed over the terrible fate of Muslim women. In this situation Muslims found themselves defending anachronistic institutions (by many Muslims' own standards) like polygamy, arguing for example that it is better to institutionalize men's polygamous desires than to force them to have secret mistresses.

Unfortunately the argument was not between the colonizers and ordinary Muslims, but between colonizers and representatives of the nationalist movement, intellectuals who had previously supported the liberation of Muslim women. Two legacies of this conflict still influence the situation of women in the Muslim world.

1. Since Western colonizers took over the paternalistic defence of Muslim women's lot, any changes in their conditions were seen as concessions to the colonizer. Since external aspects of

women's liberation like abandoning the veil for Western dress were often emulations of Western women, women's liberation was readily identified as a surrender to foreign influences.

2. The question of women's liberation has been viewed almost exclusively as a religious problem. The nationalist movement started as a religious movement, and the fight against the West was perceived very much as a modern religious crusade. The nationalists had advocated the liberation of women in the name of Islam's triumph, not in the name of any genuine modern global ideology. The eclectic variety of meanings given by kings and Palestinians and Maoists to 'Muslim socialism' demonstrates that such an ideology is still lacking.

In this book, I am not concerned with contrasting the way women are treated in the Muslim East with the way they are treated in the Christian West. I believe that sexual inequality is the basis of both systems. My aim is not to clarify which situation is better, but to understand the sexual dynamics of the Muslim world. I use comparisons between East and West only when they underline the *sui generis* pattern of the heterosexual relationship in the Muslim system.

Nor am I concerned with analysing women as an entity separate from men; rather, I try to explore the male-female relation as a component of the Muslim system, a basic element of its structure. It appears to me that the Muslim system is not so much opposed to women as to the heterosexual unit. What is feared is the growth of the involvement between a man and a woman into an all-encompassing love satisfying the sexual, emotional and intellectual needs of both partners. Such an involvement constitutes a direct threat to man's allegiance to Allah, which requires the unconditional investment of all his energies, thoughts and feelings in his God.

The change in relations between the sexes has been one of the most explosive threats that Muslim society has had to face in the twentieth century, and its dilemma has been expounded in a prolific literature concerning the relation between Islam and women.[1] Muslim societies, defeated, occupied and dominated by foreign infidel powers, have concluded that the only way to alleviate foreign domination is to free the whole Muslim 'person-power' by involving both men and women in the production process. But to achieve that aim, Muslim society would have to grant women, now needed as workers or soldiers, all the other rights which have until now been male privileges. It would have to bring about a drastic desegregation of all spheres of social life and dismantle traditional institutions which embody the inequality between the sexes.

One wonders if a desegregated society, where formerly secluded women have equal rights not only economically but sexually, would be an authentic Muslim society.

Introduction
Roots of the
Modern Situation

What was, and is still, at issue in Morocco and other Muslim societies is not an ideology of female inferiority, but rather a set of laws and customs that ensure that women's status remains one of subjugation. Prime among these are the family laws based on male authority. Although many institutions have been withdrawn from the control of religious law (business contracts for example), the family never has. The seventh-century family laws, based on male authority, were reenacted in modern legislation. The 1957 *Code du Statut Personnel*[1] (which includes all laws relating to the family) is no more than a brilliant transposition of Imam Malik's graceful and anecdotal *al-Muwatta*[2] into a series of articles, sections, and sub-sections in the concise Napoleonic tradition.

Since male modernists have recognized the necessity of altering the sexual division of labour, and since heads of Arab-Muslim states have affirmed their condemnation of sexual inequality, it seems appropriate to inquire how, and with what consequences, the emerging desire for sexual equality will be met in modern Arab-Muslim societies.

In fact, the problem seems insoluble. Women's liberation is directly linked to the political and economic conflicts rending modern Muslim societies. Every political setback generates a new necessity to liberate all the forces of development in Islamic nations. But paradoxically, every political setback inflicted by infidels generates an antithetical necessity to reaffirm the traditional Islamic nature of these societies as well. The forces of both modernity and tradition are unleashed in a single stroke and confront each other with dramatic consequences for relations between the sexes.

Let us examine more closely how this conflict works itself out symbolically in matters of policy in Morocco. Morocco claims to be modern, Arab and Muslim. Each one of these three adjectives refers to a complicated nexus of needs and aspirations, more often contradictory than complementary, which gives the modern Muslim way of life a powerful impetus and a specific character.

As a modern state Morocco is a member of the United Nations and signed the Declaration of Human Rights which stipulates, in Article 16 concerning family regulations: 'Men and women, regardless of race, nationality or religion, having reached the age of puberty, have the right to marry and establish families. They have equal rights with regard to marriage, in the marriage, and in the event of its dissolution.'

However, as a Muslim society affirming its will to keep the family under traditional Muslim law, Morocco promulgated a code that, whenever possible, dutifully respects the seventh-century *shari'a* ('divine law'). Article 12, for example, reestablishes the traditional institution of guardianship, according to which it is not the woman who gives herself in marriage, but a male guardian who gives her to her husband: 'The woman does not herself conclude the marriage act, but should have herself represented by a *wali* [guardian] whom she designates for this purpose.' Article 11 stipulates that the *wali* should be male. Another glaring violation of the Declaration of Human Rights is Article 29, which forbids a woman to choose a husband from outside the Muslim community. The marriage of a Muslim man to a non-Muslim woman, however, is not forbidden. The differences in rights and duties in marriage are so extreme that they are stated in two different articles: Article 35, 'The Rights of the Wife Towards Her Husband', and Article 36, 'The Rights of the Husband Towards His Wife'.

The actual situation in modern Muslim Morocco will appear incoherent to anyone looking for the secure and comforting logic of Cartesian 'rational behaviour'. But if we discard childish frames of mind and try to grasp the complexity of a situation in which individuals act and reflect on their actions, responding to the disconcerting demands of the world around them, then what seems incoherent becomes intelligible in its existential context. This approach is particularly important in analysing male–female dynamics in modern Morocco, where the hopes, fears and expectations of men and women are increasingly numerous and contradictory. I will scrutinize three of the imperatives of modern Muslim life that have an immediate bearing on the family structure and relations between the sexes:

1. The need for sexual equality: the Muslim male feminist movement as an effort to change the sexual division of labour.

2. The need to be Arab: Arab nationalism as a survival reflex in the face of Western domination.

3. The need to be Muslim: religion as the comforting cradle of a cosmic ideology.

The Need for Sexual Equality

The feminist movement was an expression and byproduct of Arab-Muslim nationalism. Qasim Amin (1863–1908) and Salama Musa (1887–1958) considered the liberation of women as a condition *sine qua non* for the liberation of Arab-Muslim society from the humiliating hegemony of the West. By liberation of women they meant complete equality with men in all spheres of social life. In his book *Woman Is Not the Plaything of Man*,[3] published in 1955, Salama Musa dismissed the Western example of women's liberation as particularly misleading because it did not, according to him, elevate the woman from the status of a female to the status of a human being. He urged his society to turn instead towards China and other Asian nations as better models of liberation. But here I am not so much interested in the content of the feminist movement's programme as in its genesis and causality, its instrumental aspect as part of the strategy for liberation.

A prime characteristic of Arab-Muslim society is its obsession with the West and the West's power to dominate others: 'Easterners and Westerners differ in many things . . . Among their differences is the fact that Westerners, in general, dominate the Easterners and deprive them of their cotton, rubber, copper, oil. And they beat them whenever they try to rebel.'[4]

One of the pillars of Western domination, according to the feminists, is its productiveness: 'Production in Europe and the United States is considerable and this is due to the fact that in those countries both men and women are involved in the process of production.'[5] Consequently, one of the causes of Muslim weakness is the fact that only half the nation works and produces. The other half, women, are prevented from taking part in production: 'Among the weaknesses in a society is the fact that the majority of its members are not involved in a productive work process . . . In every society women constitute half the population on average. To condemn them to be ignorant and inactive occasions the loss of half the society's productive potential and creates a considerable drain upon the society's resources.'[6]

To educate women and prepare them to take part in production is therefore a necessity if the East is to rival the West in power and productivity. Qasim Amin dismissed as idiotic theories that women do not have the same capacity and intelligence as men. He affirmed that 'If men are superior to women in physical strength and intelligence, it is because men were engaged in work activities that brought them to use their brains and bodies and therefore to develop them.'[7] He argued that once women were given the same opportunities the differences would quickly disappear.

But to include women in education and production implies sexual desegregation, and in 1895 many believed this to be against Islam and its laws: 'Many people still believe that it is not necessary to educate women. They even go so far as to think that to teach women how to read and write is against the shari'a and a violation of the divine order.'[8]

Amin tried to show that women's seclusion and their exclusion from social affairs was due not to Islam but to secular customs 'which prevailed in nations conquered by Islam and did not disappear with Islam's teaching.'[9] He affirmed that those secular traditions had been reinforced by reactionary, secular political regimes throughout the Muslim nations' history. Therefore, to change institutions that coerce women into seclusion and ignorance was not in any way an attack on or a violation of Islam. In Amin's argument, Islam becomes the most liberating of religions towards women: 'Muslim law, before any other legal system, legalized women's equality with men and asserted their freedom and liberty at times when women were still in the most debased condition in all the nations of the world. Islam granted them all human rights and recognized their legal capacity, equal to that of men in all matters . . .'[10]

When the traditionalists set out to prove the opposite, they had a rather easy task. Sheikh Ibn Murad, in a sweeping attack on a Tunisian modernist who wrote a book asserting that the liberation of women does not contradict Islam, labelled the modernist an agent of Catholic priests paid to destroy Muslim society.[11] He proceeded to establish that, indeed, Islam believes in sexual inequality: 'The meaning of marriage is the husband's supremacy . . . Marriage is a religious act . . . which gives the man a leading power over the woman for the benefit of humanity.'[12]

In this century the husband's supremacy has been seriously undermined by the effects of modernization, which has gradually thrust women out of their homes and into classrooms, offices and factories. Although sexual desegregation in Morocco has been slow and was for decades solely an upper-class urban process, it nevertheless affected the society's sexual balance seriously enough to provoke renewed claims that Islam and its laws are the everlasting guiding light in sexual matters.

The Need to be Arab
The need to reaffirm the essentially Arab nature of society, with Islam as the source of society's ideals, is dismissed as unimportant by some theoreticians of modernization. Daniel Lerner, for example, makes his task as a social scientist rather simple. After first equating modernization with Westernization, he affirms that Westernization is sweeping Baghdad and Cairo. 'Underlying the ideologies there pervades in the Middle East a sense that old ways must go because they no longer satisfy the new wants . . . Where Europeanization once penetrated only the upper level of Middle East society, affecting mainly leisure-class fashions, modernization today diffuses among a wider population and touches public institutions as well as private aspirations with its disquieting "positivist spirit".'[13]

Lerner wrote these lines in 1958, two years after the Anglo-French-Israeli attack on the Egyptian nation, at a time when demonstrations in Iraq, Syria, Jordan, Lebanon, Libya, Tunisia, Morocco, Bahrain, Qatar, Kuwait and Aden affirmed their sympathy with Egypt as an Arab nation victimized by aggression. If Lerner had listened for fifteen minutes to any Arab-Muslim radio station in the Mediterranean, he probably would have given more credit to the 'underlying ideologies' and accorded more importance to the itchy ambivalence the word 'Europeanization' provokes in both the 'leisure class' and 'the wider population.' Fortunately for social science, he noticed that 'a complication in Middle East modernization is its own ethnocentrism—expressed politically in extreme nationalism, psychologically in passionate xenophobia.'[14]

But I believe that Arab-Muslim ethnocentricity, dismissed by Lerner as a complication, is one of the most meaningful features of modernization. Being Arab and being Muslim influences institutions and sexual interaction alike.

A peculiar feature of the concept of being Arab is that many people and nations who never thought of themselves as Arab have claimed to be so since the Second World War. Nowadays being Arab is primarily a political, not a racial, claim. According to Anouar Abdel-Malek, Egyptians before the thirties took great pride in being Egyptians, the inheritors of the civilization of the ancient pharaohs, and they emphasized their difference from Arabs.[15] The predominantly Berber origin of the Moroccan population is no secret and was used for demagogic purposes by the French colonizers interested in aggravating indigenous divisions. The division between 'Berbers' and 'Arabs' was a handy one.[16] But many countries, like Egypt and Morocco, found they needed to unite as Arabs in the face of Western domination. This they did, in their distress, under the banner of Arab nationalism.

The political and cultural meaning of being Arab is clearly expressed in Allal al-Fasi's analysis of the options open to Morocco in the forties: 'Morocco must, in order to live and prosper, join a bloc of nations. Two such blocs are open for her choosing: the French Union, whose form has not yet crystallized, and the Arab Union, which has become an actual reality. In the promised French Union, Morocco will find herself—judging from past experience—in the utmost difficulties, because there is a conflict of interests and beliefs between her and France . . . Morocco is convinced that she would not be happy within this colonial union, but would remain as a storehouse for raw material and as a hatching ground for soldiers to serve France. Morocco's adherence to the Arab Union, on the other hand, would bring Morocco within this Eastern family, to which she has belonged for ten centuries and from which she had been excluded for reasons beyond her control . . .'[17]

In 1945 the Arab character of Morocco was far from evident, and Allal al-Fasi had to plead his cause to persuade the first members of the Arab League[18] to define Arab in such a way that not-so-Arab Morocco could fit the definition.[19]

History has proved Allal al-Fasi to be correct in his predictions. His party's wishes became those of the Moroccan state. Morocco, as an independent nation, became a member of the Arab League on 1 October 1958. It affirmed its Arab identity in the *Loi Fondamentale de Royaume* (June 1961), which became the basis of the 1962 constitution:

'Article 1. Morocco is an Arab and a Muslim country.

'Article 2. Islam is the official religion of the state.

'Article 3. The Arabic language is the official and national language of the state.'

The Need to be Muslim

By affirming its claim to be Arab and Muslim, Morocco expressed a view of the world based on specific aspirations and drawing its ideology from specific sources. If to be Arab implies a political and cultural choice, to choose to be Muslim implies a particular global vision of the world and a specific organization of institutions in general and of the family in particular. Islam is not merely a religion. It is a holistic approach to the world, characterized by a 'unique insistence upon itself as a coherent and closed system, a sociologically and legally and even politically organized entity in the mundane world and an ideologically organized entity as an ideal.'[20] We will now see what being Muslim implied for the Moroccan family.

In the seventh century, Muhammad created the concept of the *umma*, or 'community of believers'. There was nothing familiar about this in the minds of his contemporaries, deeply rooted in their tribal allegiances. He had to transfer the believers' allegiance from the tribe, a biological group with strong totemic overtones, to the *umma*, a sophisticated ideological group based on religious belief.[21] Islam transformed a group of individuals into a community of believers. This community is defined by characteristics that determine the relations of the individuals within the *umma* both with each other and with non-believers:

'In its internal aspect the *umma* consists of the totality of individuals bound to one another by ties, not of kinship or race, but of religion, in that all its members profess their belief in the one God, Allah, and in the mission of his prophet, Muhammad. Before God and in relation to Him, all are equal without distinction of race . . . In its external aspect, the *umma* is sharply differentiated from all other social organizations. Its duty is to bear witness to Allah in the relations of its members to one another and with all mankind. They form a single indivisible organization, charged to uphold the true faith, to instruct men in the ways of God, to persuade them to the good and to dissuade them from evil by *word and deed*.'[22]

One of the devices the Prophet used to implement the *umma* was the creation of the institutions of the Muslim family, which was quite unlike any existing sexual unions.[23] Its distinguishing feature was its strictly defined monolithic structure.

Because of the novelty of the family structure in Muhammad's revolutionary social order, he had to codify its regulations in detail. Sex is one of the instincts whose satisfaction was regulated at length by religious law during the first years of Islam. The link in the Muslim mind between sexuality and the *shari'a* has shaped the legal and ideological history of the Muslim family structure[24] and consequently of relations between the sexes. One of the most enduring characteristics of this history is that the family structure is assumed to be unchangeable, for it is considered divine.

Controversy has raged throughout this century between traditionalists who claim that Islam prohibits any change in sex roles, and modernists who claim that Islam allows for the liberation of women, the desegregation of society, and equality between the sexes. But both factions agree on one thing: Islam should remain the sacred basis of society. In this book I want to demonstrate that there is a fundamental contradiction between Islam as interpreted in official policy and equality between the sexes. Sexual equality violates Islam's premiss, actualized in its laws, that heterosexual love is dangerous to Allah's order. Muslim marriage is based on male dominance. The desegregation of the sexes violates Islam's ideology on women's position in the social order: that women should be under the authority of fathers, brothers, or husbands. Since women are considered by Allah to be a destructive element, they are to be spatially confined and excluded from matters other than those of the family. Female access to non-domestic space is put under the control of males.

Paradoxically, and contrary to what is commonly assumed, Islam does not advance the thesis of women's inherent inferiority. Quite the contrary, it affirms the potential equality between the sexes. The existing inequality does not rest on an ideological or biological theory of women's inferiority, but is the outcome of specific social institutions designed to restrain her power: namely, segregation and legal subordination in the family structure. Nor have these institutions generated a systematic and convincing ideology of women's inferiority. Indeed, it was not difficult for the male-initiated and male-led feminist movement to affirm the need for women's emancipation, since traditional Islam recognizes equality of potential. The democratic glorification of the human individual, regardless of sex, race, or status, is the kernel of the Muslim message.

In Western culture, sexual inequality is based on belief in women's biological inferiority. This explains some aspects of Western women's liberation movements, such as that they are almost always led by women, that their effect is often very superficial, and that they have not yet succeeded in significantly changing the male-female dynamics in that culture. In Islam there is no such belief in female inferiority. On the contrary, the whole system is based on the assumption that women are powerful and dangerous beings. All sexual institutions (polygamy, repudiation, sexual segregation, etc.) can be perceived as a strategy for containing their power.

This belief in women's potence is likely to give the evolution of the relationship between men and women in Muslim settings a pattern entirely different from the Western one. For example, if there are any changes in the sex status and relations, they will tend to be more radical than in the West and will necessarily generate more tension, more conflict, more anxiety, and more aggression. While the women's liberation movement in the West focuses on women and their claim for equality with men, in Muslim countries it would tend to focus on the mode of relatedness between the sexes and thus would probably be led by men and women alike. Because men can see how the oppression of women works against men, women's liberation would assume the character of a generational rather than sexual conflict. This could already be seen in the opposition between young nationalists and old traditionalists at the beginning of the century, and currently it can be seen in the conflict between parents and children over the dying institution of arranged marriage.

At stake in Muslim society is not the emancipation of women (if that means only equality with men), but the fate of the heterosexual unit. Men and women were and still are socialized to perceive each other as enemies. The desegregation of social life makes them realize that besides sex, they can also give each other friendship and love. Muslim ideology, which views men and women as enemies, tries to separate the two, and empowers men with institutionalized means to oppress women. But whereas fifty years ago there was coherence between Muslim ideology and Muslim reality as embodied in the family system, now there is a wide discrepancy between that ideology and the reality that it pretends to explain. This book explores many aspects of that discrepancy and describes the *sui generis* character of male-female dynamics in Morocco, one of the most striking mixtures of modernity and Muslim tradition.

The *umma* is a simultaneously social and religious group, and the problem of the relation between secular and divine power inevitably arises. Islam solves it by unequivocally subordinating the secular to the religious authority and by denying the secular authority the right to legislate.[25] H.A.R. Gibb noted:

'The head of the *umma* is Allah, and Allah alone. His rule is immediate and his commands, as revealed in Muhammad, embody the Law and Constitution of the *umma*. Since God is himself the Sole Legislator, there can be no room in Islamic political theory for legislation or legislative powers, whether enjoyed by a temporal ruler or by any kind of assembly. There can be no sovereign state, in the sense that the state has the right to enact its own law, though it may have some freedom in determining its constitutional structure. The law precedes the state, both logically and in terms of time, and the state exists for the sole purpose of maintaining and enforcing the law.'[26]

In a word, the Muslim's allegiance is not to a secular power, be it the state or its legislators, but to the *shari'a*, which transcends both humanity and temporality. The fact that God is the legislator gives the legal system a specific configuration. First, it denies the existence of human legislation: 'Strictly speaking, Islamic theory does not recognize the possibility of human legislation and that which the human rules must make regulations for carrying the divine law into effect.'[27] Second, it asserts the inalterability of the law and its eternal hold on human action: 'The *shari'a* . . . is universally accepted as the Law of God. God, at any rate so far as human experience of him may presume to go, is unchanging and to a pious mind this may appear to imply that his law is also unchangeable.'[28] Third, it extends the scope of the law to matters which usually belong to other spheres: 'Law, then, in any sense in which a Western lawyer will recognize the term, is but part of the whole Islamic system, or rather it is not even a part but one of several inextricably combined elements thereof. *Shari'a*, the Islamic term which is commonly rendered in English by 'Law', is rather "the whole duty of man", moral and pastoral theology and ethics, high spiritual aspirations and the detailed ritualistic and formal observance which to some minds is a vehicle for such aspirations and to others a substitute for it, all aspects of law: public and private hygiene and even courtesy and good manners are all part and parcel of the *shari'a*.'[29]

Is it correct to say, then, that the Muslim world did not develop a modern legal system in the Western sense of the word? Are the laws governing public and private actions of Muslims today the same laws sketched by Muhammad? Of course not. The *shari'a* had to confront the daily realities of the increasingly numerous and culturally diverse members of the *umma*. Schools of law were gradually created and specialists of law appeared. They endeavoured to extrapolate and interpret the divine principles in order to meet the earthly needs of the believer in his day-to-day life.

The result was a gradual liberation of some subjects from the hold of religious law. Joseph Schacht distinguishes two kinds of legal subject matter in Islamic law.[30] First, subject matter upon which the *shari'a* failed to maintain its hold: penal law, taxation, constitutional law, law of war and law of contracts and obligations. Second, subject matter upon which the hold of the *shari'a* was uncontested for centuries and in some areas is uncontested even today: purely religious duties, family law (marriage, divorce, maintenance), law of inheritance and law of endowments for religious institutions. These have been, and still are, closely connected with religion and are therefore still ruled by the *shari'a*.

Interference by the state in any matter seen to be within the domain of the *shari'a* presupposes acceptance of the Western idea of sovereign secular power. Schacht writes: 'Whereas a traditional Muslim ruler must, by definition, remain the servant of the Sacred Law of Islam, a modern government, and particularly a parliament with the modern idea of sovereignty behind it, can constitute itself its master.'[31] Even though impregnated with the Western concept of sovereign secular power, the Muslim *umma*, through the traditionalist supporters of the sovereignty of the *shari'a*, strongly resisted the intervention of modern legislators in family law.

Historical Interests Behind Modern Legislation

Modern legislation in the Muslim world did not spring from any new ideological conception of the individual and society, as had been the case in Muhammad's seventh-century revolutionary Muslim order. Modern legislation was initiated and carried out by the colonial powers[32] and after independence was continued by the independent nation states. In both cases, the interests of the individual in general and of women in particular were secondary if not irrelevant compared with the interests of the powers involved.

The colonial powers were motivated to intervene in Muslim

legislation not by idealistic concern for the natives, but by their own economic interests. This was the case of the Anglo-Muhammadan Law in India from 1772 onward and the *Droit Musulman* in Algeria from 1830 onward.

The psychological result of the foreign powers' intervention in Muslim legislation was to transform the *shari'a* into a symbol of Muslim identity and the integrity of the *umma*. Modern changes were identified as the enemy's subtle tools for carrying out the destruction of Islam.

When the Muslim states became independent, modern legislation was not initiated in the interests of the masses. The new laws were closely connected with the battle between traditional law practitioners and modernists, who were mostly lawyers in the Western sense of the word.[33] It was not only a battle between two different conceptions of law, but also a clash of interests between two groups of professionals. The new laws forced the traditional 'lawyers' to give up some of their power, and their profits, to the young modernist lawyers.

The Moroccan nationalist movement never made the transition from an independence movement to a nation-building movement. After having 'driven the foreigners out', the nationalists proved unable to transform their ideology and political apparatus into an instrument for social change. According to the Moroccan historian Abdallah Laroui, the creativity of the nationalist movement as a producer of ideas for change died out years before independence. He buries it in 1930–32.[34] Nor did any other group among those that played important roles from the mid-fifties to the mid-seventies offer a coherent set of solutions to the country's problems.

The main feature of post-independence policy seems to be empiricism, *ad hoc* decision-making, rather than the subordination of decisions to a long-term programme of action.[35] The immediate interests of the independent nation states were the determining factors motivating the legislators. Their inability to generate a genuine modern ideology made family legislation directly dependent on traditional ideologies and contemporary contingencies, whence its inconsistency.[36]

The absence of a genuine modern ideology strengthened the hold of Islam as the only coherent ideology that masses and rulers could refer to. It is therefore not surprising that Morocco, like other independent Muslim states, recognized Islam as the ideology of the family in its otherwise Western-inspired *Code*.

The law of 1957 creating the commission charged with the task of writing a Muslim code was justified thus: 'Considering that the Kingdom of Morocco is going through a period characterized by deep changes in all matters and especially in legislative matters; considering that Muslim law constitutes an eminently delicate matter susceptible to many interpretations; considering the absolute necessity, therefore, of gathering the rules of this law into a code so as to facilitate its teaching as well as its application . . . we have decided on the creation of a commission entrusted with the task of elaborating the Muslim code of personal status.'[37]

The *Code du Statut Personnel* stipulates that in all cases that cannot be resolved by reference to the *Code*, the source to turn to for guidance is the jurisprudence of the Malekite school.[38] The founder of the Malekite school, Imam Malik Ibn Anas, was an Arab who lived in Medina and was a judge in the eighth century. In two chapters of his *Muwatta*, one on marriage, the other on divorce, he spelled out the basis for the institution of the family. There is more than an inspirational similarity between Malik's *Muwatta* and the Moroccan *Code du Statut Personnel*. The idea prevailing in Malik's time that sexuality is a religious matter to be regulated by divine laws seems to be one of the concepts modern legislators did not question at all.

The seventh-century concept of sexuality, as embodied in the modern family laws, conflicts dramatically with the sexual equality and desegregation fostered by modernization. In the first part of this book I want to explore, through early Muslim sources, the Muslim ideology of the sexes as revealed by the institution of the family. In the second part, I will analyse, through my data and other sources of information on the present situation, the modernizing trend as embodied in women's gradual acquisition of the right to be educated and to compete for jobs. I will look especially closely at the effects of modernization on male-female interaction both inside and outside the family.

PART ONE

The Traditional Muslim View of Women and Their Place in the Social Order

1
The Muslim Concept of Active Female Sexuality

The Function of Instincts

The Christian concept of the individual as tragically torn between two poles—good and evil, flesh and spirit, instinct and
reason—is very different from the Muslim concept. Islam has a
more sophisticated theory of the instincts, more akin to the
Freudian concept of the libido. It views the raw instincts as
energy. The energy of instincts is pure in the sense that it has
no connotation of good or bad. The question of good and bad
arises only when the social destiny of men is considered. The
individual cannot survive except within a social order. Any
social order has a set of laws. The set of laws decides which uses
of the instincts are good or bad. It is the use made of the
instincts, not the instincts themselves, that is beneficial or
harmful to the social order. Therefore, in the Muslim order it is
not necessary for the individual to eradicate his instincts or to
control them for the sake of control itself, but he must use them
according to the demands of religious law.

> When Muhammad forbids or censures certain human
> activities, or urges their omission, he does not want them
> to be neglected altogether, nor does he want them to be
> completely eradicated, or the powers from which they
> result to remain altogether unused. He wants those powers
> to be employed as much as possible for the right aims.
> Every intention should thus eventually become the right
> one and the direction of all human activities one and the
> same.[1]

Aggression and sexual desire, for example, if harnessed in the right direction, serve the purposes of the Muslim order; if suppressed or used wrongly, they can destroy that very order:

> Muhammad did not censure wrathfulness with the intention of eradicating it as a human quality. If the power of wrathfulness were no longer to exist in man, he would lose the ability to help the truth to become victorious. There would no longer be holy war or glorification of the word of God. Muhammad censured the wrathfulness that is in the service of Satan and reprehensible purposes, but the wrathfulness that is one in God and in the service of God deserves praise.[2]
>
> . . . Likewise when he censures the desires, he does not want them to be abolished altogether, for a complete abolition of concupiscence in a person would make him defective and inferior. He wants the desire to be used for permissible purposes to serve the public interests, so that man becomes an active servant of God who willingly obeys the divine commands.[3]

Imam Ghazali (1050–1111) in his book *The Revivification of Religious Sciences*[4] gives a detailed description of how Islam integrated the sexual instinct in the social order and placed it at the service of God. He starts by stressing the antagonism between sexual desire and the social order: 'If the desire of the flesh dominates the individual and is not controlled by the fear of God, it leads men to commit destructive acts.'[5] But used according to God's will, the desire of the flesh serves God's and the individual's interests in both worlds, enhances life on earth and in heaven. Part of God's design on earth is to ensure the perpetuity of the human race, and sexual desires serve this purpose:

> Sexual desire was created solely as a means to entice men to deliver the seed and to put the woman in a situation where she can cultivate it, bringing the two together softly in order to obtain progeny, as the hunter obtains his game, and this through copulation.[6]

He created two sexes, each equipped with a specific anatomic configuration which allows them to complement each other in the realization of God's design.

> God the Almighty created the spouses, he created the man with his penis, his testicles and his seed in his kidneys [kidneys were believed to be the semen-producing gland]. He created for it veins and channels in the testicles. He gave the woman a uterus, the receptacle and depository of the seed. He burdened men and women with the weight of sexual desire. All these facts and organs manifest in an eloquent language the will of their creator, and address to every individual endowed with intelligence an unequivocal message about the intention of His design. Moreover, Almighty God did clearly manifest His will through his messenger (benediction and salvation upon him) who made the divine intention known when he said 'Marry and multiply'. How then can man not understand that God showed explicitly His intention and revealed the secret of His creation? Therefore, the man who refuses to marry fails to plant the seed, destroys it and reduces to waste the instrument created by God for this purpose.[7]

Serving God's design on earth, sexual desire also serves his design in heaven.

> Sexual desire as a manifestation of God's wisdom has, independently of its manifest function, another function: when the individual yields to it and satisfies it, he experiences a delight which would be without match if it were lasting. It is a foretaste of the delights secured for men in Paradise, because to make a promise to men of delights they have not tasted before would be ineffective. . . . This earthly delight, imperfect because limited in time, is a powerful motivation to incite men to try and attain the perfect delight, the eternal delight and therefore urges men to adore God so as to reach heaven. Therefore the desire to reach the heavenly delight is so powerful that it helps men to persevere in pious activities in order to be admitted to heaven.[8]

Because of the dual nature of sexual desire (earthly and heavenly) and because of its tactical importance in God's strategy, its regulation had to be divine as well. In accordance with God's interests, the regulation of the sexual instinct was one of the key devices in Muhammad's implementation on earth of a new social order in then-pagan Arabia.

Female Sexuality: Active or Passive?

According to George Murdock, societies fall into two groups with respect to the manner in which they regulate the sexual instinct. One group enforces respect of sexual rules by a 'strong internalization of sexual prohibitions during the socialization process', the other enforces that respect by 'external precautionary safeguards such as avoidance rules', because these societies fail to internalize sexual prohibitions in their members.[9] According to Murdock, Western society belongs to the first group while societies where veiling exists belong to the second.

> Our own society clearly belongs to the former category, so thoroughly do we instil our sex mores in the consciences of individuals that we feel quite safe in trusting our internalized sanctions. . . . We accord women a maximum of personal freedom, knowing that the internalized ethics of premarital chastity and post-marital fidelity will ordinarily suffice to prevent abuse of their liberty through fornication or adultery whenever a favourable opportunity presents itself. Societies of the other type . . . attempt to preserve premarital chastity by secluding their unmarried girls or providing them with duennas or other such external devices as veiling, seclusion in harems or constant surveillance.[10]

However, I think that the difference between these two kinds of societies resides not so much in their mechanisms of internalization as in their concept of female sexuality. In societies in which seclusion and surveillance of women prevail, the implicit concept of female sexuality is active; in societies in which there are no such methods of surveillance and coercion of women's behaviour, the concept of female sexuality is passive.

In his attempt to grasp the logic of the seclusion and veiling of women and the basis of sexual segregation, the Muslim feminist Qasim Amin came to the conclusion that women are better able to control their sexual impulses than men and that consequently sexual segregation is a device to protect men, not women.[11]

He started by asking who fears what in such societies. Observing that women do not appreciate seclusion very much and conform to it only because they are compelled to, he concluded that what is feared is *fitna*: disorder or chaos. (*Fitna* also means a beautiful woman—the connotation of a *femme fatale* who makes men lose their self-control. In the way Qasim Amin used it *fitna* could be translated as chaos provoked by sexual disorder and initiated by women.) He then asked who is protected by seclusion.

> If what men fear is that women might succumb to their masculine attraction, why did they not institute veils for themselves? Did men think that their ability to fight temptation was weaker than women's? Are men considered less able than women to control themselves and resist their sexual impulse? . . . Preventing women from showing themselves unveiled expresses men's fear of losing control over their minds, falling prey to *fitna* whenever they are confronted with a non-veiled woman. The implications of such an institution lead us to think that women are believed to be better equipped in this respect than men.[12]

Amin stopped his inquiry here and, probably thinking that his findings were absurd, concluded jokingly that if men are the weaker sex, they are the ones who need protection and therefore the ones who should veil themselves.

Why does Islam fear *fitna*? Why does Islam fear the power of female sexual attraction over men? Does Islam assume that the male cannot cope sexually with an uncontrolled female? Does Islam assume that women's sexual capacity is greater than men's?

Muslim society is characterized by a contradiction between what can be called 'an explicit theory' and 'an implicit theory' of female sexuality, and therefore a double theory of sexual dynamics. The explicit theory is the prevailing contemporary belief that men are aggressive in their interaction with women, and women are passive. The implicit theory, driven far further into the Muslim unconscious, is epitomized in Imam Ghazali's classical work.[13] He sees civilization as struggling to contain women's destructive, all-absorbing power. Women must be controlled to prevent men from being distracted from their social and religious duties. Society can survive only by creating institutions that foster male dominance through sexual segregation and polygamy for believers.

The explicit theory, with its antagonistic, machismo vision of relations between the sexes is epitomized by Abbas Mahmud al-Aqqad.[14] In *Women in the Koran* Aqqad attempted to describe male-female dynamics as they appear through the Holy Book. Aqqad opened his book with the quotation from the Koran establishing the fact of male supremacy ('the men are superior to them by a degree') and hastily concludes that 'the message of the Koran, which makes men superior to women is the manifest message of human history, the history of Adam's descendants before and after civilization.'[15]

What Aqqad finds in the Koran and in human civilization is a complementarity between the sexes based on their antagonistic natures. The characteristic of the male is the will to power, the will to conquer. The characteristic of the female is a negative will to power. All her energies are vested in seeking to be conquered, in wanting to be overpowered and subjugated. Therefore, 'She can only expose herself and wait while the man wants and seeks.'[16]

Although Aqqad has neither the depth nor the brilliant systematic deductive approach of Freud, his ideas on the male-female dynamic are very similar to Freud's emphasis on the 'law of the jungle' aspect of sexuality. The complementarity of the sexes, according to Aqqad, resides in their antagonistic wills and desires and aspirations.

> Males in all kinds of animals are given the power—embodied in their biological structure—to compel females

to yield to the demands of the instinct (that is, sex). . . .
There is no situation where that power to compel is given
to women over men.[17]

Like Freud, Aqqad endows women with a hearty appetite for
suffering. Women enjoy surrender.[18] More than that, for Aqqad
women experience pleasure and happiness only in their subjugation, their defeat by males. The ability to experience
pleasure in suffering and subjugation is the kernel of femininity, which is masochistic by its very nature. 'The woman's
submission to the man's conquest is one of the strongest
sources of women's pleasure.'[19] The machismo theory casts the
man as the hunter and the woman as his prey. This vision is
widely shared and deeply ingrained in both men's and women's
vision of themselves.

The implicit theory of female sexuality, as seen in Imam
Ghazali's interpretation of the Koran, casts the woman as the
hunter and the man as the passive victim. The two theories
have one component in common, the woman's *qaid* power ('the
power to deceive and defeat men, not by force, but by cunning
and intrigue'). But while Aqqad tries to link the female's *qaid*
power to her weak constitution, the symbol of her divinely
decreed inferiority, Imam Ghazali sees her power as the most
destructive element in the Muslim social order, in which the
feminine is regarded as synonymous with the satanic.

The whole Muslim organization of social interaction and
spacial configuration can be understood in terms of women's
qaid power. The social order then appears as an attempt to
subjugate her power and neutralize its disruptive effects. The
opposition between the implicit and the explicit theories in
Muslim society would appear clearly if I could contrast Aqqad
and Imam Ghazali. But whereas the implicit theory is brilliantly
articulated in Imam Ghazali's systematic work on the institution of marriage in Islam, the explicit theory has an unfortunate
advocate in Aqqad, whose work is an amateurish mixture of
history, religion and his own brand of biology and anthro-
pology. I shall therefore contrast Imam Ghazali's conception of
sexual dynamics not with Aqqad's but with that of another
theoretician, one who is not a Muslim but who has the

advantage of possessing a machismo theory that is systematic in the elaboration of its premises—Sigmund Freud.

Imam Ghazali vs. Freud: Active vs. Passive

In contrasting Freud and Imam Ghazali we are faced with a methodological obstacle, or rather what seems to be one. When Imam Ghazali was writing the chapter on marriage in his book *The Revivification of Religious Sciences*, in the eleventh century, he was endeavouring to reveal the true Muslim belief on the subject. But Freud was endeavouring to build a scientific theory, with all that the word 'scientific' implies of objectivity and universality. Freud did not think that he was elaborating a European theory of female sexuality; he thought he was elaborating a universal explanation of the human female. But this methodological obstacle is easily overcome if we are 'conscious of the historicity of culture'.[20] We can view Freud's theory as a 'historically defined' product of his culture. Linton noted that anthropological data has shown that it is culture that determines the perception of biological differences and not the other way around.

> All societies prescribe different attitudes and activities to men and to women. Most of them try to rationalize these prescriptions in terms of the physiological differences between the sexes or their different roles in reproduction. However, a comparative study of the statuses ascribed to women and men in different cultures seems to show that while such factors may have served as a starting point for the development of a division, the actual prescriptions are almost entirely determined by culture. Even the psychological characteristics ascribed to men and to women in different societies vary so much that they can have little physiological basis.[21]

A social scientist works in a biographically determined situation in which he finds himself 'in a physical and socio-cultural environment as defined by him, within which he has his position, not merely his position in terms of physical space and outer time or of his status and role within the social system but also his moral and ideological position.'[22] We can therefore consider Freud's theory of sexuality in general, and of female sexuality in particular, as a reflection of his society's beliefs and not as a scientific (objective and ahistorical) theory. In comparing Freud and Imam Ghazali's theories we will be comparing the two different cultures' different conceptions of sexuality, one based on a model in which the female is passive, the other on one in which the female is active. The purpose of the comparison is to highlight the particular character of the Muslim theory of male-female dynamics, and not to compare the condition of women in the Judeo-Christian West and the Muslim East.

The novelty of Freud's contribution to Western contemporary culture was his acknowledgement of sex (sublimated, of course) as the source of civilization itself. The rehabilitation of sex as the foundation of civilized creativity led him to the reexamination of sex differences. This reassessment of the differences and of the consequent contributions of the sexes to the social order yielded the concept of female sexuality in Freudian theory.

In analysing the differences between the sexes, Freud was struck by a peculiar phenomenon—bisexuality—which is rather confusing to anyone trying to assess sex differences rather than similarities:

> Science next tells you something that runs counter to your expectations and is probably calculated to confuse your feelings. It draws your attention to the fact that portions of the male sexual apparatus also appear in women's bodies, though in an atrophied state, and vice-versa in the alternative case. It regards their occurrence as indications of bisexuality as though an individual is not a man or a woman but always both—merely a certain amount more one than the other.[23]

The deduction one expects from bisexuality is that anatomy cannot be accepted as the basis for sex differences. Freud made this deduction:

You will then be asked to make yourself familiar with the idea that the proportion in which masculine and feminine are mixed in an individual is subject to quite considerable fluctuations. Since, however, apart from the very rarest cases, only one kind of sexual product, ova or semen, is nevertheless present in one person, you are bound then to have doubts as to the decisive significance of those elements and must conclude that what constitutes masculinity or femininity is an unknown characteristic which anatomy cannot lay hold of.[24]

Where then did Freud get the basis for his polarization of human sexuality into a masculine and a feminine sexuality, if he affirms that anatomy cannot be the basis of such a difference? He explains this in a footnote, apparently considering it a secondary point:

It is necessary to make clear that the conceptions 'masculine' and 'feminine', whose content seems so unequivocal to the ordinary meaning, belong to the most confused terms in science and can be cut up into at least three paths. One uses masculinity and femininity at times in the sense of activity and passivity, again in the biological sense and then also in the sociological sense. The first of these three meanings is the essential one and the only one utilizable in psychoanalysis.[25]

The polarization of human sexuality into two kinds, feminine and masculine, and their equation with passivity and activity in Freudian theory helps us to understand Imam Ghazali's theory, which is characterized precisely by the absence of such a polarization. It conceives of both male and female sexuality partaking of and belonging to the same kind of sexuality.

For Freud, the sex cells' functioning is symbolic of the male-female relation during intercourse. He views it as an antagonistic encounter between aggression and submission.

The male sex cell is actively mobile and searches out the female and the latter, the ovum, is immobile and waits passively. . . . This behaviour of the elementary sexual organism is indeed a model for the conduct of sexual individuals during intercourse. The male pursues the female for the purpose of sex union, seizes hold of her and penetrates into her.[26]

For Imam Ghazali, both the male and female have an identical cell. The word sperm (*ma'*, 'water drop') is used for the female as well as for the male cell. Imam Ghazali referred to the anatomic differences between the sexes when clarifying Islam's position on coitus interruptus (*'azl*), a traditional method of birth control practised in pre-Islamic times. In trying to establish the Prophet's position on *'azl*, Imam Ghazali presented the Muslim theory of procreation and the sexes' contribution to it and respective roles in it.

> The child is not created from the man's sperm alone, but from the union of a sperm from the male with a sperm from the female . . . and in any case the sperm of the female is a determinant factor in the process of coagulation.[27]

The puzzling question is not why Imam Ghazali failed to see the difference between the male and female cells, but why Freud, who was more than knowledgeable about biological facts, saw the ovum as a passive cell whose contribution to procreation was minor compared to the sperm's. In spite of their technical advancement, European theories clung for centuries to the idea that the sperm was the only determining factor in the procreation process; babies were prefabricated in the sperm[28] and the uterus was just a cozy place where they developed.

Imam Ghazali's emphasis on the identity between male and female sexuality appears clearly in his granting the female the most uncontested expression of phallic sexuality, ejaculation. This reduces the differences between the sexes to a simple difference of pattern of ejaculation, the female's being much slower than the male's.

> The difference in the pattern of ejaculation between the sexes is a source of hostility whenever the man reaches

> his ejaculation before the woman. . . . The woman's ejacu-
> lation is a much slower process and during that process
> her sexual desire grows stronger and to withdraw from her
> before she reaches her pleasure is harmful to her.[29]

Here we are very far from the bedroom scenes of Aqqad
and Freud, which resemble battlefields more than shelters of
pleasure. For Imam Ghazali there is neither aggressor nor
victim, just two people cooperating to give each other pleasure.

The recognition of female sexuality as active is an explosive
acknowledgement for the social order with far-reaching implications for its structure as a whole. But to deny that male and
female sexuality are identical is also an explosive and decisive
choice. For example, Freud recognizes that the clitoris is an
evident phallic appendage and that the female is consequently
more bisexual than the male.

> There can be no doubt that the bisexual disposition which
> we maintain to be characteristic of human beings manifests
> itself much more plainly in the female than in the male.
> The latter has only one principal sexual zone—only one
> sexual organ—whereas the former has two: the vagina,
> the true female organ, and the clitoris, which is analogous
> to the male organ.[30]

Instead of elaborating a theory which integrates and elaborates the richness of both sexes' particularities, however, Freud
elaborates a theory of female sexuality based on reduction: the
castration of the phallic features of the female. A female child,
bisexual in infancy, develops into a mature female only if she
succeeds in renouncing the clitoris, the phallic appendage: 'The
elimination of the clitorial sexuality is a necessary pre-condition
for the development of femininity.'[31] The pubertal development
process brings atrophy to the female body while it enhances the
phallic potential of the male's, thus creating a wide discrepancy
in the sexual potential of humans, depending on their sex:

> Puberty, which brings to the boy a great advance of libido,
> distinguishes itself in the girl by a new wave of repression

which especially concerns the clitoral sexuality. It is a part of the male sexual life that sinks into repression. The reinforcement of the inhibitions produced in the woman by the repression of puberty causes a stimulus in the libido of the man and forces it to increase its capacity; with the height of the libido, there is a rise in the over-estimation of the sexual, which can be present in its full force only when the woman refuses and denies her sexuality.[32]

The female child becomes a woman when her clitoris 'acts like a chip of pinewood which is utilized to set fire to the harder wood.'[33] Freud adds that this process takes some time, during which the 'young wife remains anesthetic'.[34] This anesthesia may become permanent if the clitoris refuses to relinquish its excitability. The Freudian woman, faced with her phallic partner, is therefore predisposed to frigidity.

The sexual frigidity of women, the frequency of which appears to confirm this disregard (the disregard of nature for the female function) is a phenomenon that is still insufficiently understood. Sometimes it is psychogenic and in that case accessible to influence; but in other cases it suggests the hypothesis of its being constitutionally determined and even of being a contributory anatomical factor.[35]

By contrast with the passive, frigid Freudian female, the sexual demands of Imam Ghazali's female appear truly over-whelming, and the necessity for the male to satisfy them becomes a compelling social duty: 'The virtue of the woman is a man's duty. And the man should increase or decrease sexual intercourse with the woman according to her needs so as to secure her virtue.'[36] The Ghazalian theory directly links the security of the social order to that of the woman's virtue, and thus to the satisfaction of her sexual needs. Social order is secured when the woman limits herself to her husband and does not create *fitna*, or chaos, by enticing other men to illicit intercourse. Imam Ghazali's awe of the overpowering sexual demands of the active female appears when he admits how difficult it is for a man to satisfy a woman.

> If the prerequisite amount of sexual intercourse needed by the woman in order to guarantee her virtue is not assessed with precision, it is because such an assessment is difficult to make and difficult to satisfy.[37]

He cautiously ventures that the man should have intercourse with the woman as often as he can, once every four nights if he has four wives. He suggests this as a limit, otherwise the woman's sexual needs might not be met.

> It is just for the husband to have sexual intercourse with his wife every four nights if he has four wives. It is possible for him to extend the limit to this extreme. Indeed, he should increase or decrease sexual intercourse according to her own needs.[38]

Freud's and Ghazali's stands on foreplay are directly influenced by their visions of female sexuality. For Freud, the emphasis should be on the coital act, which is primarily 'the union of the genitals',[39] and he deemphasizes foreplay as lying between normal (genital) union and perversion, which consists '. . . in either an anatomical transgression of the bodily regions destined for sexual union or a lingering at the intermediary relations to the sexual object which should normally be rapidly passed on the way to definite sexual union.'[40]

In contrast, Imam Ghazali recommends foreplay, primarily in the interest of the woman, as a duty for the believer. Since the woman's pleasure necessitates a lingering at the intermediary stages, the believer should strive to subordinate his own pleasure, which is served mainly by the genital union.

> The Prophet said, 'No one among you should throw himself on his wife like beasts do. There should be, prior to coitus, a messenger between you and her.' People asked him, 'What sort of messenger?' The Prophet answered, 'Kisses and words.'[41]

The Prophet indicated that one of the weaknesses in a man's character would be that

> . . . he will approach his concubine-slave or his wife and that he will have intercourse with her without having prior to that been caressing, been tender with her in words and gestures and laid down beside her for a while, so that he does not harm her, by using her for his own satisfaction, without letting her get her satisfaction from him.[42]

The Fear of Female Sexuality

The perception of female aggression is directly influenced by the theory of women's sexuality. For Freud the female's aggression, in accordance with her sexual passivity, is turned inward. She is masochistic.

> The suppression of woman's aggressiveness which is prescribed for them constitutionally and imposed on them socially favours the development of powerful masochistic impulses, which succeed, as we know, in binding erotically the destructive trends which have been diverted inwards. Thus masochism, as people say, is truly feminine. But if, as happens so often, you meet with masochism in men, what is left for you but to say that these men exhibit very plainly feminine traits.[43]

The absence of active sexuality moulds the woman into a masochistic passive being. It is therefore no surprise that in the actively sexual Muslim female aggressiveness is seen as turned outward. The nature of her aggression is precisely sexual. The Muslim woman is endowed with a fatal attraction which erodes the male's will to resist her and reduces him to a passive acquiescent role. He has no choice; he can only give in to her attraction, whence her identification with *fitna*, chaos, and with the anti-divine and anti-social forces of the universe.

The Prophet saw a woman. He hurried to his house and had intercourse with his wife Zaynab, then left the house and said, 'When the woman comes towards you, it is Satan who is approaching you. When one of you sees a woman and he feels attracted to her, he should hurry to his wife. With her, it would be the same as with the other one.'[44]

Commenting on this quotation, Imam Muslim, an established voice of Muslim tradition, reports that the Prophet was referring to the

... fascination, to the irresistible attraction to women God instilled in man's soul, and he was referring to the pleasure man experiences when he looks at the woman, and the pleasure he experiences with anything related to her. She resembles Satan in his irresistible power over the individual.[45]

This attraction is a natural link between the sexes. Whenever a man is faced with a woman, *fitna* might occur: 'When a man and a woman are isolated in the presence of each other, Satan is bound to be their third companion.'[46]

The most potentially dangerous woman is one who has experienced sexual intercourse. It is the married woman who will have more difficulties in bearing sexual frustration. The married woman whose husband is absent is a particular threat to men: 'Do not go to the women whose husbands are absent. Because Satan will get in your bodies as blood rushes through your flesh.'[47]

In Moroccan folk culture this threat is epitomized by the belief in Aisha Kandisha, a repugnant female demon. She is repugnant precisely because she is libidinous. She has pendulous breasts and lips and her favourite pastime is to assault men in the streets and in dark places, to induce them to have sexual intercourse with her, and ultimately to penetrate their bodies and stay with them for ever.[48] They are then said to be inhabited. The fear of Aisha Kandisha is more than ever present in Morocco's daily life. Fear of the castrating female is a legacy of tradition and is seen in many forms in popular beliefs and practices and in both religious and mundane literature, particularly novels.

Moroccan folk culture is permeated with a negative attitude towards femininity. Loving a woman is popularly described as a form of mental illness, a self-destructive state of mind. A Moroccan proverb says

> Love is a complicated matter
> If it does not drive you crazy, it kills you.[49]

The best example of this distrust of women is the sixteenth-century poet Sidi Abderahman al-Majdoub. His rhymes are so popular that they have become proverbs.

> Women are fleeting wooden vessels
> Whose passengers are doomed to destruction.

Or

> Don't trust them [women], so you would not be betrayed
> Don't believe in their promises, so you would not be deceived
> To be able to swim, fish need water
> Women are the only creatures who can swim without it.[50]

And finally

> Women's intrigues are mighty
> To protect myself I run endlessly
> Women are belted with serpents
> And bejewelled with scorpions.[51]

The Muslim order faces two threats: the infidel without and the woman within.

> The Prophet said, 'After my disappearance there will be no greater source of chaos and disorder for my nation than women.'[52]

The irony is that Muslim and European theories come to the same conclusion: women are destructive to the social order—for Imam Ghazali because they are active, for Freud because they are not.

Different social orders have integrated the tensions between religion and sexuality in different ways. In the Western Christian experience sexuality itself was attacked, degraded as animality and condemned as anti-civilization. The individual was split into two antithetical selves: the spirit and the flesh, the ego and the id. The triumph of civilization implied the triumph of soul over flesh, of ego over id, of the controlled over the uncontrolled, of spirit over sex.

Islam took a substantially different path. What is attacked and debased is not sexuality but women, as the embodiment of destruction, the symbol of disorder. The woman is *fitna*, the epitome of the uncontrollable, a living representative of the dangers of sexuality and its rampant disruptive potential. We have seen that Muslim theory considers raw instinct as energy which is likely to be used constructively for the benefit of Allah and His society if people live according to His laws. Sexuality *per se* is not a danger. On the contrary, it has three positive, vital functions. It allows the believers to perpetuate themselves on earth, an indispensable condition if the social order is to exist at all. It serves as a 'foretaste of the delights secured for men in Paradise',[53] thus encouraging men to strive for paradise and to obey Allah's rule on earth. Finally, sexual satisfaction is necessary to intellectual effort.

The Muslim theory of sublimation is entirely different from the Western Christian tradition as represented by Freudian psychoanalytic theory. Freud viewed civilization as a war against sexuality.[54] Civilization is sexual energy 'turned aside from its sexual goal and diverted towards other ends, no longer sexual and socially more valuable'.[55] The Muslim theory views civilization as the outcome of satisfied sexual energy. Work is the result not of sexual frustration but of a contented and harmoniously lived sexuality.

> The soul is usually reluctant to carry out its duty because duty [work] is against its nature. If one puts pressures on

the soul in order to make it do what it loathes, the soul rebels. But if the soul is allowed to relax for some moments by the means of some pleasures, it fortifies itself and becomes after that alert and ready for work again. And in the woman's company, this relaxation drives out sadness and pacifies the heart. It is advisable for pious souls to divert themselves by means which are religiously lawful.[56]

According to Ghazali, the most precious gift God gave humans is reason. Its best use is the search for knowledge. To know the human environment, to know the earth and galaxies, is to know God. Knowledge (science) is the best form of prayer for a Muslim believer. But to be able to devote his energies to knowledge, man has to reduce the tensions within and without his body, avoid being distracted by external elements, and avoid indulging in earthly pleasures. Women are a dangerous distraction that must be used for the specific purpose of providing the Muslim nation with offspring and quenching the tensions of the sexual instinct. But in no way should women be an object of emotional investment or the focus of attention, which should be devoted to Allah alone in the form of knowledge-seeking, meditation, and prayer.

Ghazali's conception of the individual's task on earth is illuminating in that it reveals that the Muslim message, in spite of its beauty, considers humanity to be constituted by males only. Women are considered not only outside of humanity but a threat to it as well. Muslim wariness of heterosexual involvement is embodied in sexual segregation and its corollaries: arranged marriage, the important role of the mother in the son's life, and the fragility of the marital bond (as revealed by the institutions of repudiation and polygamy). The entire Muslim social structure can be seen as an attack on, and a defence against, the disruptive power of female sexuality.

2
Regulation of Female Sexuality in the Muslim Social Order

It is a widely shared belief among historians in different cultures that human history is progressive, that human society, in spite of accidents and setbacks, moves progressively from 'savagery' to 'civilization'. Islam too has a progressive vision of history. The year 622, the *hijra*, is the year one of civilization. Before the *hijra* was *jahiliya*, the time of barbarism, the time of ignorance.[1] Islam maintains that one of the dimensions of society in which there was progress is human sexuality.[2] Under *jahiliya* sexuality was promiscuous, lax, and uncontrolled, but under Islam it obeys rules. The specific, unique code of Islam's law outlaws fornication as a crime. But what is peculiar about Muslim sexuality as civilized sexuality is this fundamental discrepancy: if promiscuity and laxity are signs of barbarism, then only women's sexuality was civilized by Islam; male sexuality is promiscuous (by virtue of polygamy) and lax (by virtue of repudiation).[3] This contradiction is evident in both seventh-century family legislation and the modern Moroccan Code.

Polygamy

Decree No. 2-57-1040 of August 1957 charged a commission of ten men with the elaboration of a Muslim Moroccan code of law, the *Muduwana*, or *Code du Statut Personnel*. These ten men re-enacted polygamy, whose basis is a famous verse of the Koran.

> Marry of the women who seem good to you, two, three, or four, and if ye fear that ye cannot do justice [to so many] then one [only] . . .

A notable peculiarity of this verse is that the only condition limiting a man's right to polygamy is fear of injustice, a subjective feeling not easy to define legally. The Moroccan legislators, probably aware of the rather outmoded aspect of polygamy, rephrased the verse in such a way that the word 'forbidden' closely follows 'polygamy', but the content is identical.

Art. 30: If injustice is feared, polygamy is forbidden.

This echoes verse 129 of the fourth sura: 'You cannot be perfectly equitable to all your wives, even if you so desire.'

The Koran does not provide a justification for polygamy, but Ghazali does. According to him, polygamy is based on instinct. Ghazali's justification clearly reveals the flaw in the Muslim theory of sexuality, and provides one of the most telling insights into the problem that modern Morocco, as a Muslim society, is obliged to solve. Polygamy entitles the male not simply to satisfy his sexuality, but to indulge it to saturation without taking women's needs into consideration, women being con-sidered simply 'agents' in the process.

> Once the agent [of sexual excitation] is known, the remedy should be adapted to its intensity and degree, the aim being to relieve the soul from tension. One can decide for a greater number [of women] or a lesser number . . . for the man burdened with a strong sexual desire and for whom one woman is not enough to guarantee his chastity [chastity for a married person being abstention from *zina*, fornication], it is recommended that he add to the first wife, others. The total should not exceed, however, four.[4]

Polygamy implies that a man's sexual drive might require copulation with more than one partner to relieve his soul (and body) from sexual tension. Elsewhere Ghazali implies that there is no difference of character between male and female sex drives. Thus he unintentionally acknowledges a latent reason for women's reluctant attitude towards the Muslim order.

Men and women are considered to have similar instinctual drives, yet men are entitled to as many as four partners to satisfy those drives, while women must content themselves with at most one man, and sometimes as little as a quarter of one. Since saturation of the sexual impulse for males requires polygamy, one can speculate that fear of its inverse—one woman with four husbands—might explain the assumption of women's insatiability, which is at the core of the Muslim concept of female sexuality. Since Islam assumes that a sexually frustrated individual is a very problematic believer and a troublesome citizen of the *umma*, the distrust of women, whose sexual frustration is organized institutionally, is even greater.

Polygamy also has a psychological impact on the self-esteem of men and women. It enhances men's perception of themselves as primarily sexual beings and emphasizes the sexual nature of the conjugal unit. Moreover, polygamy is a way for the man to humiliate the woman as a sexual being; it expresses her inability to satisfy him. For Moroccan folk wisdom, this function of polygamy as a device to humiliate the woman is evident: 'Debase a woman by bringing in [the house] another one.'[5]

The verse of the Koran justifying polygamy also grants men the right, without any condition or limit, to possess as many concubines as 'your right hand possess'. But the Moroccan legislators, taking into account the budget difficulties of the contemporary believer, said nothing about the institution of concubinage, which died out in Morocco with the disappearance of female slavery at the beginning of the twentieth century. (My grandmother was kidnapped in Chaouia plain, sold in Fez, and bore my mother as a concubine to a member of the landowning urban bourgeoisie, then politically and financially powerful. This group was the main buyer of female slaves for decades after the French occupation in 1912.)

Repudiation

Though polygamy is mentioned only once in the Koran, repudiation is the subject of many long and detailed verses. Those most commonly referred to are in the second sura.

Verse 227: And if ye decide upon divorce [remember that] Allah is hearer, knower.

Verse 229: Divorce must be pronounced twice, and then a woman must be retained in honour or released in kindness.

But legally speaking, the most significant reference to the institution of repudiation is probably verse 20 of the fourth sura, which reveals the basic capriciousness of the male decision to sever the marital bond.

And if ye wish to exchange one wife for another and ye have given into one of them a sum of money (however great) take nothing from it.

The words 'wish' and 'exchange' are the key elements in the Muslim institution of verbal repudiation, whose characteristic is the unconditional right of the male to break the marriage bond without any justification, and without having his decisions reviewed by a court or a judge. In reenacting the seventh-century institution, the Moroccan Code limits the judge's role simply to registering the husband's decision.

Art. 46: Repudiation can be performed either verbally or in writing, or by signs and gestures if the husband is an illiterate man, or deprived of the capacity of speech.
Art. 80: The *adouls* [Muslim court officials] issue a repudiation act as soon as they are asked to do so.

Like polygamy, repudiation has an instinctual basis, but whereas polygamy deals with the intensity of the male's sexual drive, repudiation deals with its instability. Repudiation prevents the male from losing his sexual appetite through boredom. It aims at ensuring a supply of new sexual objects, within the framework of marriage, to protect him against the temptation of *zina*.

If God by His goodness and grace facilitates man's life [by allowing him to be polygamous] and that man attains thus the peace of heart by them [women], that is good. If not, the changing process is recommended.[6]

This recommendation was acted upon by such exemplary men as Hasan, the Prophet's grandson.

It has been said that Hasan Ibn Ali was a marriage addict. He married 200 wives. Sometimes he'd marry four at a time; he'd repudiate four at a time and marry new ones. Muhammad (benediction and salvation upon him) said to Hasan, 'You resemble me physically and morally.' . . . It has been said that this proclivity to marry is often precisely one of the similarities between Hasan and the messenger of God (benediction and salvation upon him).[7]

The somewhat ridiculous aspect of repudiation did not escape Allah himself, who warned the believer entrusted with the power to break the marital bond with a mere spoken formula not to make 'the revelations of Allah a laughing-stock [by your behaviour].'[8]

The right to polygamy and repudiation granted exclusively to males seems to have been an innovation in seventh-century Arabia. Historical evidence indicates that earlier marriage patterns had been more varied and less codified. Some forms of marriage implied that the woman had a right to self-determination in choosing a husband or dismissing him. Indeed, the Prophet himself, despite his powerful attraction as a triumphant military leader and successful statesman, was himself faced with female sexual self-determination. He was solicited in marriage by many women and was rejected by many as well.

The Prophet's life is not a simple historical document in Islam. The detailed record of his thoughts and deeds is, after the Koran, which is the word of God, the prime source of the teachings that shape and guide the believer's life. The Prophet's life is an example of how a Muslim should deal with and find solutions to his daily problems. It is the guiding light for overcoming obstacles according to the Muslim ideal.

The Prophet's Experience
of Female Self-Determination

The Prophet's marital life seems to be symbolic of the transition Arabia was undergoing. He lived for 62 years (born AD 570 of the Christian calendar, he died in 632). He married for the first time in the year 595 and with his first wife, Khadija, had a monogamous marriage that lasted twenty-five years, until her death in 620. It was only then that the Prophet started a new marital life, and in a span of twelve years (620–632) he married twelve women, arranged three other marriages which did not take place, and rejected several female suitors who asked for his hand, or rather 'offered themselves', according to the consecrated Muslim formula.[9]

The first woman who asked to marry him was his first wife, Khadija Bint Khuwalid, a wealthy and active woman of the Quraish tribe who invested her fortune in the trade caravans then flourishing in Mecca. She employed Muhammad to accompany one of her caravans and was so impressed by his trustworthiness that she decided to marry him. He was then twenty-five years old, and it was his first marriage. She was forty, and it was her third. She bore all his children (four daughters and two sons who died young), except for Ibrahim, the son of Maria, his Coptic concubine.[10]

Among the women who offered themselves to the Prophet were Umm Sharik, whose proposal he did not accept, and Leila Bint al-Khatim, whose proposal he did accept. But the latter marriage did not take place, because Leila was discouraged by her tribe. Her people convinced her that her proud temperament was ill-suited for the accommodations a polygamous marriage requires.

The lack of ritual surrounding such a move by a woman is illustrated by a dialogue between the Prophet and Leila.

> She came to the Prophet (upon him Allah's peace and prayer), who was sitting talking to another man, and who did not see her coming, until he felt her hand on him. He said, 'Who are you?' She said, 'I am Leila Bint al-Khatim. I come to you to offer myself. Will you marry me?' He said, 'I accept.'[11]

For a woman to decide to initiate a sexual union seems to have been a casual gesture made by the woman herself, without reference to her father or male relatives. Although Leila's kin discouraged her marriage, they did so not as authorities, but as persuasive counsellors concerned about her well-being. She decided not to marry the Prophet not because she was coerced, but because she was convinced by their argument about the Prophet's other wives and her inability to cope with them.

Hiba ('the act by which a woman gives herself to a man') was outlawed after the Prophet died.[12] If he was the last Arab man to be chosen freely by women, he was also probably the last to be repudiated by them.

There were several women with whom the Prophet contracted marriages that were never consummated.[13] In three cases the marriage was broken by a repudiation formula pronounced by the woman. Some reports say that she repeated the formula three times. (This makes it look identical to the repudiation formula institutionalized by Islam as a man's privilege: if the man pronounces it three times, the divorce is definite; if he pronounces it once or twice only, the marital bond is suspended for some weeks, after which the husband can resume his marriage.)

Every time the formula was pronounced by the woman, the Prophet covered his face with his sleeve, left the nuptial room and asked for the woman to be returned to her tribe immediately. It appears that repudiation, like *hiba*, was characterized by a lack of ritual, which leads me to think that it was a rather common occurrence.

> When she [Asma Bint al-Numan] entered the room where he [the Prophet] was, he closed the door and released the curtain. When he thrust his hand towards her, she said, 'I take refuge in Allah from thee.' The Prophet immediately covered his head with his sleeve and said, 'You are granted such a protection', three times. He then left her and gave orders for her to be returned to her tribe.[14]

Similar incidents happened with Mulaika Bint Ka'ab and Fatima Bint al-Dahhak.[15]

Muslim sources give many versions of the motives that led these three women to behave as they did. The most common explanation is that the three of them, who all belonged to tribes different from that of the Prophet, were deceived by their co-wives.[16] The Quraishite wives of the Prophet (led of course by Aisha, the indefatigable, vivacious beloved of the Prophet), threatened by the three women's beauty and exoticism, instructed the newcomers to pronounce the formula 'so that the Prophet would love them more'. Victims of deceit, according to these versions, the three tribal women were surprised by the Prophet's reaction.

I think these rather heavy-handed versions of the story are the work of Muslim historians who thought it necessary to disguise the embarrassing fact that the Prophet had been rejected and 'repudiated'. It is hard to believe that three women, from different tribes and with different personalities, were equally gullible and equally easily deceived by their rivals in exactly the same way. Once perhaps. But three times? One report says explicitly that the woman rejected the Prophet because she did not like him.[17] This is a much more likely reason. At least two of the women, Asma and Mulaika, were famous for their beauty.[18] They were young. The Prophet was in his early sixties, and—a very important point—he was polygamous. For women like Asma, who was herself from a princely tribe, [19] the Prophet's prestige as a leader would not make him very desirable if what he had to give her was shared with more than nine colleagues. But the explanation of their behaviour is secondary here. What we are interested in is the fact that in the Prophet's time there was a customary formula by which a woman could dismiss her husband. The Prophet's phobic behaviour (having to leave her immediately) after the woman pronounced the formula shows that this was so.

If a woman could dismiss her husband at will, then she possessed substantial independence and self-determination. The Muslim social order was vehemently opposed to self-determination for women and declared that only men could repudiate their spouses.

The fear of female self-determination is basic to the Muslim order and is closely linked to fear of *fitna*. If women are not constrained, then men are faced with an irresistible sexual attraction that inevitably leads to *fitna* and chaos by driving them to *zina*, illicit copulation. The Prophet's own experience of the corrosive attraction of female sexuality underlies much of the Muslim attitude towards women and sexuality. Fear of succumbing to the temptation represented by women's sexual attraction—a fear experienced by the Prophet himself—accounts for many of the defensive reactions to women by Muslim society.

The Prophet's Experience of the Irresistible Attraction of Women

The Prophet's interactions with women, his intimate quarrels with his wives, his behaviour with the women he loved, are the basis for many legal features of the Muslim family structure. One of the striking aspects of his interaction with women is the contradiction between the ideals he preached as a model for Muslim believers when dealing with women and the way he actually dealt with them himself. One of those ideals is what should motivate a man to marry.

> The Prophet said that the woman can be married for her religion [Muslim faith], for her fortune, or her beauty. Be motivated in your choice by her religion.[20]

Although many of his marriages were motivated by religious and political considerations (politics, after all, is religion in Islam), such as the need for tribal alliances, many of them were motivated solely by the woman's beauty.

His marriage to the Jewish woman Safiya Bint Huyay could not possibly have been motivated by the need for an alliance, the Jews being his defeated enemies at the time. Moreover, when Safiya was captured by Muslim soldiers after the defeat of her people, it was not evident that she, as part of the booty, would fall to Muhammad since booty was shared according to the democratic, customary rules of Arab raiding. One report mentions that Safiya was allotted to a soldier called Dahia but that when the Prophet heard of her 'incomparable beauty' he sent for Dahia, paid him Safiya's price, and freed her before marrying her.[21]

His marriage to another Jewish woman, Rayhana Bint Zayd, could not have been motivated by alliance either. Like Safiya, she belonged to a Jewish tribe, was captured after her people's defeat, and was known to be 'a beautiful woman'.[22] But unlike Safiya, her marital status is contested; some reports say that she was kept as a concubine and never became a wife of the Prophet.

Maria the Copt, a famous beauty, was given as a gift from Egypt to the Prophet.[23] He had intercourse with her as a concubine, and she bore him a son, Ibrahim, who died in infancy. The Prophet's desire for Maria was so strong that it led him to violate another of his ideals: that a man should be just in his dealings with his wives. A man should keep strictly to the rotation schedule and not have intercourse with a wife, even if he so desired, if it was not her day. Hafsa, one of the Prophet's wives, however, caught him having intercourse with Maria in Safiya's room on Safiya's day. 'O Prophet of God, in my room and on my day!' fulminated Safiya angrily. Afraid of the anger of his other wives, and especially of his most beloved Aisha, he promised Hafsa never to touch Maria again if she would keep the incident secret.[24] But she spoke out, and the Prophet received orders from God to retract his promise; he then resumed relations with Maria.[25] Maria's power over the Prophet is best described in Aisha's words:

> I never was as jealous as I was of Maria. That is because she was a very beautiful, curly-haired woman. The Prophet was very attracted to her. In the beginning, she was living near us and the Prophet spent entire days and nights with her until we protested and she became frightened.[26]

The Prophet then decided to transfer Maria to a more secure dwelling far from his legitimate wives, and kept seeing her in spite of their pressure.

Another woman the Prophet married for her beauty (although

in this case alliance was a motive as well) was Juwariya Bint al-Harith who was, according to Aisha's description, 'so beautiful that whoever caught a glimpse of her fell in love with her'.[27] According to Aisha, the main motive of the Prophet's marriage to Juwariya was physical attraction.

> The Prophet was in my room when Juwariya came to ask him about a contract. By God, I hated her when I saw her coming towards him. I knew that he was going to see what I saw [her beauty].[28]

Another instance of the effect of female beauty on the Prophet was that of Dubaa Bint Amr, who 'was among the most beautiful of Arab women. . . . Her hair was long enough to cover all her body.'[29] The Prophet heard of her beauty, went to her son, and asked him if he could marry his mother. The son, following the custom in such instances, told the Prophet that he would have to ask his mother's opinion. He did, and she was so excited about the prospect of such a union that she told her son that he should have given her in marriage right away, that it was impolite of him to have placed any condition on the Prophet's legitimate desire. But when the son went to the Prophet with the hope that the subject of his mother would be discussed, the Prophet never brought it up again. He had heard meanwhile that although she was indeed beautiful, she was also ageing.

But the most significant example of women's irresistible power over the Prophet is probably his sudden (and scandalous, by his own people's standards) passion for Zainab Bint Jahsh,[30] the wife of his adopted son Zaid. In Muhammad's Arabia, the link created by adoption was considered identical to blood-ties. Moreover, Zainab was the Prophet's own cousin, and the Prophet himself had arranged her marriage with his adopted son.

One morning Muhammad went to his adopted son's house to ask after him. When he saw Zainab, who was half-dressed, he felt an irresistible passion for her. She had hurried to the door to let the Prophet know that her husband was not in. She was surprised when he declined her invitation to come in, and instead ran off, mumbling prayers. When she reported the incident to her husband, he went to his adopted father to say that he was prepared to divorce Zainab if the Prophet wanted to marry her. The Prophet refused Zaid's proposition until God revealed his order to Muhammad to marry Zainab.

> . . . And thou didst hide in thy mind that which Allah was to bring to light, and thou didst fear mankind whereas Allah had a better right that thou shouldst fear Him. So when Zaid had performed the necessary formality [of divorce] from her, We have her unto thee in marriage, so that [henceforth] there may be no sin for believers in respect to wives of their adopted sons, when the latter have performed the necessary formality [of release] from them. The commandment of Allah must be fulfilled.[31]

To calm the scandalized clamour of the Prophet's contemporaries, the Muslim God made a lasting change in the institution of adoption. Verse four of the thirty-third sura denied that adoption creates legal and relational ties between individuals. Article 83 of the Moroccan *Code* reenacted the Koran's decision: 'Adoption confers neither legal status nor the rights of parenthood.'

It should be noted here that the Muslim Prophet's heroism does not lie in any relation of aggression, conquest, or exercise of brute force against women, but on the contrary in his vulnerability. It is because he is vulnerable, and therefore human, that his example has exerted such power over generations of believers. The Prophet was anything but macho in today's sense of behaving as a conqueror of women in the way described by Abbas Mahmud al-Aqqad, the sole respectable masculine role in the Muslim Mediterranean today. The Prophet's behaviour leads us to recognize the complexity of masculine reality. He achieved his colossal task on earth not because he was outstandingly aggressive and rigid, but because he was vulnerable and able to recognize his vulnerability, to acknowledge it and take it into account. The most striking example of this is his admission of his overwhelming love for Aisha, who was not yet eighteen years old when he died in his sixties.

The Prophet was striving to achieve justice between his wives in whatever he gave them and he dutifully respected the rotation system [one night each], but he used to say, 'God, this is as far as I can go in controlling my inclinations. I have no power over what you own and I don't [meaning his heart].' Aisha was the one he loved the most and all his other wives knew that.[32]

The power of women over men has dictated many of the Muslim laws concerning marriage. Men have a right to sexual satisfaction from their wives so that they will be less vulnerable to the attraction of other women. And women must be sexually satisfied so that they do not try to tempt other men to fornication.

The Need to Ensure Sexual Satisfaction

Sexual satisfaction for both partners is seen as necessary to prevent adultery. For example *muhsan*, which means 'to protect', legally means both 'marriage' and 'chastity', because a married person should be 'protected' from adultery by satisfying his desires within the marriage. Under penal law, the *muhsan* receives a harsher punishment than an unmarried person who commits illicit sexual intercourse.[33]

The word *zina* means illicit intercourse—'any sexual intercourse between two persons who are not in a state of legal matrimony or concubinage.'[34] *Zina* covers both fornication (involving unmarried people) and adultery (involving at least one married individual, a *muhsan*). Before Islam, *zina* was not considered a sin, a crime against religion. With Islam, it became a crime against God, His laws, and the established order.

Zina was one of the practices the Muslim recruits were required to renounce. The ritual by which new female converts were admitted into the Muslim community included a pledge to respect the six demands known as the woman's oath of allegiance.

O Prophet! If believing women come unto thee, taking oath of allegiance unto thee that they (1) will ascribe nothing as partner unto Allah, and will (2) neither steal, (3) nor commit *zina*, (4) nor kill their children, (5) nor produce any lie that they have devised between their hands and feet, (6) nor disobey thee in what is right, then accept their allegiance and ask Allah to forgive them[35] [numbers mine].

As a protective device against *zina*, marriage is highly recommended to believers of both sexes. A sexually frustrated member of the community is considered dangerous. This is the main reason why Islam is opposed to asceticism and requires believers with pious and saintly vocations to acquire pious wives. Abstinence and celibacy are vehemently discouraged.[36] Atika Bint Zaid, a woman who decided to live as a celibate after her husband's death, was discouraged from doing so by the Caliph Umar, who went so far as to propose marriage to her.[37]

Islam socializes sexual intercourse through the institution of marriage within the framework of the family. The only legitimate sexual intercourse is between married people. Marriage should guarantee sexual satisfaction for husband and wife and protect both partners against seeking satisfaction outside it. The institution of marriage penalizes the husband or the wife who fails to provide sexual services for his or her spouse.

If the wife refuses to have intercourse with her husband she is penalized both on earth and in heaven. The Prophet, according to Imam Bukhari, said a woman 'who is asked by her husband to join him in bed and refuses to do so is condemned by the angels who hurl anathema on her until the daybreak.'[38] Although having savage swarms of angels set against one is a rather unsettling thought, the most effective device for bringing the woman to respond sexually to her husband is material. Muslim law grants the husband whose wife refuses his advances the right to withhold maintenance (food, clothing and lodging), which it is normally his duty to provide. The 1958 Moroccan *Code* safeguards this right for male citizens.

> Article 123: The non-pregnant woman who abandons the conjugal community or refuses to have sexual intercourse with her husband may retain her right to maintenance but

the judge has the right to suspend her right to maintenance if he commands the woman to return to the conjugal abode or to regain the conjugal bed and she refuses to obey. She has no right of appeal against the judge's decision as long as she does not execute his order.

The availability of sexual intercourse is vital to the man's protection against *zina* because, as we have seen from the Prophet's example, the only way to resist another woman's illicit attraction is to rush to your wife.

This need to protect the man is probably the reason why, even though menstruation is defined as polluting,[39] a husband is allowed to approach his menstruating wife so long as he avoids penetration. Imam Ghazali explains that the husband can ask his wife to cover her body between the navel and the knee with a cloth and to masturbate him with her hands.[40]

Parallel to the protection of the man against the wife's whimsical or biological obstacles, there are many legal devices to ensure the woman's sexual satisfaction by her husband. Although the right of the woman to ask the judge to pronounce a divorce is limited to a very few grounds, sex is one of them. The woman has the right to ask the judge to initiate divorce if she can testify that her husband is impotent. While Malik decided that the woman should wait one year before asking for a divorce on these grounds,[41] the modern Moroccan legislators thought it an urgent matter and urged the judge to respond immediately by releasing the woman if she files for divorce on grounds of her husband's impotence.[42]

Another form of divorce justified by lack of sexual satisfaction is *ila*. If the husband makes an oath to abstain from having sexual intercourse with his wife for four months and if he keeps his oath, she can demand a divorce from the judge.[43] The Moroccan *Code* reenacted *ila* in Article 58, which identifies it as a legitimate basis upon which a woman can initiate divorce proceedings (*al-tatliq*).

The compelling duty to provide sexual satisfaction is intelligible only if one is reminded of the fear of unrestrained female sexuality. Curbing active female sexuality, preventing female sexual self-determination, is the basis of many of Islam's family institutions.

Remnants of Pre-Muslim Sexual Practices

Two techniques of divorce that have survived in Muslim marriages are reminiscent of female self-determination under *jahiliya*, although the woman's power to dissolve her marriage is now subordinated to the judge's decision and approval. The two techniques are *tamlik* and *khul'*, both of which can be considered as survivals of, or transitional compromises with, women's former freedom in marriage contracts.

The techniques of *tamlik* confer upon the wife the power to divorce her husband if he delegates such power to her. The repudiation formula, 'I divorce thee', becomes 'I divorce thee whenever thou decides it'.

Imam Malik explains the logic of this technique: 'If a man gives his wife the right to self-determination (*mallakaha amraha*), whatever she decides becomes legally binding.'[44] If she decides to leave him, there is nothing he can do about it. He recounts the dialogue between a Muslim judge and a Muslim husband painfully surprised to see his wife use the power he had delegated to her.

> The man: I gave my wife the right to self-determination and she divorced me. What do you think?
> The judge: I think that what she did is perfectly legal.
> The man: Please do not do that [i.e., agree with her against me].
> The judge: I did not do that, you did it.[45]

The *tamlik* procedure was not reenacted in the 1958 Moroccan *Code*, which specifies that 'repudiation subordinated to a condition is valueless'.[46] The *tamlik* had subordinated repudiation to the wife's approval. The technique of *tamlik* is interesting because of the mechanisms and concepts involved in it, especially the concept of self-determination as something that can be transferred from the man to the woman. It expressed the idea that the woman's freedom of decision is not an inseparable privilege of the husband, but can be the object of bargaining between the spouses.

Khul' literally means 'to cast off'. Legally it refers to the husband's renouncing his rights over the woman as a wife after she has agreed to pay him a certain sum of money to buy her freedom. Imam Malik mentions that it was practised in the Prophet's time.[47] The buying of a woman's freedom is often used in cases in which it is evidently the woman's·fault that the marriage is not working. A price is negotiated between the husband and the woman's family and is paid to the unlucky husband.

Schacht sees *khul'* as 'an exchange of assets'. [48] It seems to be a fair practice by which everybody gets something: the woman her freedom and the man compensation for his loss. But it is easy to imagine the corruption of such a practice into a weapon to oppress women. If a wife has a fortune of her own or comes from a wealthy family, the man may make life so miserable for her that she will have to 'buy herself' back from him.

Such cases must have been quite frequent, because Malik warns that if it is established that the woman was coerced by her husband, the judge should free her and the husband should not be granted indemnization.[49] The Moroccan *Code* institutionalizes the *khul'* technique in Articles 58 and 61. Article 63 warns, 'The husband shall acquire compensation only if the wife has consented to obtain her divorce without coercion or constraint.'

Tamlik and *khul'* are remnants of women's sexual self-determination before Islam. But most other features of pre-Muslim sexual practices were stamped out by the rules regulating Muslim marriages. Before Islam, for example, women frequently remarried as soon as they were divorced. If pregnant by their first husband, the child was considered to belong to the second husband.[50] Physical paternity was regarded as unimportant. Under Islam physical paternity was essential, so women were forbidden to remarry until several months had passed and it became evident that they were not pregnant by their previous husband.

Idda: The Muslim Guarantee of Paternity

One of the first definitions of paternity in Arabia was the proverb, 'the child belongs to the bed', a succinct statement of the Muslim belief. The child born in wedlock belongs to the husband, even if he is not the biological father. A pregnant married woman is assumed to have been impregnated by her husband, and the child belongs to him.

The idea that a woman impregnated by a believer would engage in intercourse with another believer, even in the framework of marriage, became sacrilege: 'Whoever believes in Allah and in the other world would not allow his sperm to water another man's child.'[51]

A woman who is pregnant is therefore forbidden to enter into a new marriage until she gives birth to the child: 'For those [women] with child, the waiting period shall be till they bring forth their burden.'[52]

Islam ensured physical paternity by instituting the *idda* period, which obliges a widowed or divorced woman to wait several menstrual cycles before getting married again.[53] Widows are required to wait four months and ten days, divorcees four months.[54]

The Moroccan *Code* reenacts the *idda* just as it was established in the Koran and adopted by Malik. Article 72 forbids a pregnant woman to marry before her child's birth. Article 73 obliges the repudiated wife to wait three consecutive menstrual flows before engaging in a new marital union. But further measures are taken, in specific cases, to plug any loopholes in the system of paternity.

Even menopausal women do not go unchecked. On the off chance that they can still conceive, they have to wait three months before seeking a new husband (Article 73). Given the volatile tendencies of marriage markets in Muslim society and their competitiveness (due precisely to repudiation, which makes available a greater number of marriageable women than demography alone would), the *idda* constitutes a rather harsh penalty for all newly divorced women and in particular for menopausal women who have the further disadvantage of being middle-aged in a society in which youth is avidly prized.

The penalizing aspect of the *idda* appears even more clearly in the case of women whose menstrual flow is irregular or who have no flow at all. On this point there is a significant difference between the Koran and the leader of the Malekite school. The

Moroccan *Code* emulates the latter. While the Koran requires only a three-month waiting period for those 'who despair of menstruation'[55] or have doubts about its regularity, Imam Malik penalizes those two groups with a waiting period of twelve months.[56] Article 73 of the Moroccan *Code* also stipulates that 'women whose menstrual flow is late or irregular, or who cannot distinguish between one menstrual flow and the following, should wait an *idda* period of twelve months.'

The new social structure of Islam, which constituted a revolution in the mores of pre-Islamic Arabia, was based on male dominance. Polygamy, repudiation, the prohibition of *zina*, and the guarantees of paternity were all designed to foster the transition from a family based on some degree of female self-determination to a family based on male control. The Prophet saw the establishment of the male-dominated Muslim family as crucial to the establishment of Islam. He bitterly fought existing sexual practices where marital unions for men and women alike were unstable and lax.

3
Sex and Marriage
Before Islam

Marriage on the Eve of Islam

The marriage practices of the first Muslim communities, richly documented by Arab sources, provide much information about the sexual practices that prevailed in pre-Islamic Arabia. But the wealth of information contained in Arab documentation highlights the paucity of analysis of the data.

Ideological biases have often inhibited more audacious analytical efforts. Historians dealing with these problems are often so deeply imbued with centuries of monotheistic patriarchy that they find it impossible even to imagine that the situation on the eve of Islam was far more complex than the system later consolidated by Islam. The important thing is not whether a patriarchal or matriarchal system held sway in pre-Islamic Arabia; the real question is rather to discover which sexual practices Islam forbade and which it encouraged. It is by retracing Islam's *selective* attitude toward *jahiliya* sexual practices that we may grasp the new religion's stance toward relations between the sexes. That is my object here.

The point, then, is not patriarchy or matriarchy, but to what extent the Muslim family represented a continuation of the pre-Islamic family. Was there a radical break with the practices and principles of the old family or not?

It is interesting to note the sharp differences of opinion on this matter among various historians depending on the era in which they wrote. Historians of the first few centuries of Islam generally exhibited a far more open and flexible attitude than their modern colleagues. Early Islamic historians like Bukhari (author of the *Sahih*), Ibn Habib al-Baghdadi (*Kitab al-*

Muhabbar), and Ibn Saad (*Kitab al-Takabat*) held that the Muslim family marked a break with earlier practices. They acknowledged that the patriarchal marriage endorsed by Islam had been paralleled by many other forms of union that were clearly anti-patriarchal: there were unions in which the child did not belong to the biological father (and even polyandrous marriages in which the woman had more than one regular sexual partner), and there were unions in which the woman had an absolute right to send her husband away if she so desired, severing the marital bond with a ritual gesture as simple as lowering a veil across the mouth of her tent when she no longer wished her husband to enter. But all these practices, though amply documented, were subsequently prohibited by Islam.

The rigidity with which modern Arab historians refuse to admit, even at the level of pure analysis, that customs expressing female sexual self-determination could have existed is truly fascinating. The most extreme case is perhaps Salah Ahmad al-'Ali. Although he has collected abundant evidence about pre-Islamic sexual customs (and his knowledge of both Arab documents, and documents and studies unearthed by orientalists is erudite) that proves the existence of unions in which the woman's sexual self-determination was absolute and unchallengeable, he asserts that 'bedouin society was organized according to the patrimonial system in which the man had power and authority over the woman, the children before puberty, and the household.'[1] He claims that *mut'a* and *mubada'a* marriages were considered deviant practices (*shaddah*) during the pre-Islamic period (see Bukhari's comments on pre-Islamic marriages later in this chapter).[2]

I have read the same Arab sources as he has, and nowhere have I found clear information on the statistical frequency of these pre-Islamic marital practices or on the moral attitude of pre-Islamic society to them. Earlier historians simply noted that Islam condemned all marriage customs that contradicted the religion's principles, namely the principles of patriarchy. It is therefore of some interest to look briefly at what these customs and practices were. Exactly what was it that Islam forbade? According to my reading of the historical evidence, Islam banished all practices in which the sexual self-determination of women was asserted.

Muslim marriage gave absolute male authority a stamp of holy approval. One source of data on marriage in early Islam is the eighth volume of the *Kitab al-Tabaqat al-Kubra* ('*The Book of Great Classes*') by Ibn Saad.[3] The work as a whole is a classification of the early Muslim community. The eighth volume, *On Women*, is a compilation of biographical information about the first women converts to join the Prophet's entourage. The first part of the book contains information on women related to the Prophet either by blood or marriage ties: his female cousins, aunts, daughters, and wives. The second part is a compilation of biographical data on 574 women who were among the first converts.

A systematic analysis of Ibn Saad's book was undertaken in 1939 by Gertrude Stern in order to assess marriage in the early Muslim community.[4] She did not try to interpret her findings or to make them fit any particular theory. Her work is therefore a mere description of marriage processes: betrothal, consent, guardianship, dowry, adultery, and the dissolution of marriage ties. She found no 'fixed institution of marriage'. She describes a diversity of sexual unions whose 'outstanding feature appears to be the looseness of marriage ties in general and the lack of any legal system for regulating procedure.'[5]

> If one takes into consideration the preceding facts in conjunction with other factors such as the absence of any contract or legal guardian, the exclusion of the wife from her husband's inheritance, the easy methods of divorce, the lack of a period of seclusion after divorce and widowhood—the *idda*—the conclusion must be reached that there was no fixed institution of marriage and that marriage ties were in no sense regarded as binding.[6]

The work of Gertrude Stern is impressive in its rigorous attempt at objectivity and strict analysis of the data, yet her assertion that 'there was no idea of a fixed institution of marriage' can be misleading. This can mean either that there was no fixed institution of marriage at all or that there was no institution of marriage similar to models Stern considered stable. The difference is enormous. From her description it seems likely that what she meant was that there was no fixed and meticulously regulated institution similar to the juridically complex procedure of Muslim marriage.

According to Ibn Saad's biographical data, polygamy existed neither in Mecca, a sophisticated urban centre with trading relations reaching deep into the Byzantine world, nor in Medina, the basically agrarian community to which the Prophet emigrated. Stern wrote:

> There is no reliable evidence of the practice of polygamy in pre-Islamic times at al-Madinah [Medina], as understood in the Islamic era, that is, the system of a man marrying a number of women and maintaining them in one or more establishments. . . . Moreover, from a study of the genealogical tables which I have compiled, it is to be observed that there is no indication of a well-defined system of polygamy.[7]

She arrived at identical conclusions for Mecca, adding:

> It is possible that Meccan men contracted marriages with tribal women, but that they were either of a temporary character or the woman remained with her own people, but as is the case of the Medinans there is no evidence of a man supporting and maintaining more than one wife at a time.[8]

Here Gertrude Stern draws attention to a vital detail usually overlooked in the analysis of pre-Islamic marriages: the uxorilocal character of the marriage.[9] Polygamy in an uxorilocal setting is an altogether different institution from polygamy in a virilocal one. Uxorilocal polygamy could very well co-exist with a similar polyandrous right of the woman, who might be visited by many men.

The Prophet's great-grandfather, Hashim, contracted an uxorilocal marriage. The offspring of the union, the Prophet's grandfather, Abd al-Muttalib, was raised by his mother.[10]

Hashim (who was from Mecca) contracted the union during a trip to the town of Medina, where he asked Salama Bint Amr for her hand and married her. She bore him Abd al-Muttalib. Hashim left Medina and went back to Mecca, leaving the child behind with its mother. After Hashim's death, his brother went to Medina to fetch the boy, then an adolescent. It took three days of negotiations between Salama and the uncle to decide the fate of the child, who said that he would leave his mother only if she herself ordered him to do so. Salama is described as a woman who

> ... because of her noble birth and her high position among her people, never allowed herself to marry anyone except under the condition that she would be her own master and retain the initiative to leave her husband if she disliked him.[11]

Muslim historians link sexual self-determination to the woman's high social position.[12] Al-Baghdadi's *Kitab al-Muhabbar* contains a chapter entitled 'Women who kept complete autonomy after their marriage, who stayed with their husband if they wanted and left him if such was their desire, and who behaved in this manner because of their prestigious position (*qadrihinna*) and their high rank (*sharafuhunna*).' The names of women of the Arab aristocracy then follow, with Salama Bint Amr heading the list. It is understandable that Ibn Hisham, the historian of the *Sira* ('biography') of the Prophet, would seek some justification other than matriliny to explain Salama's attitude, since matriliny was condemned as prostitution by the time the *Sira* was written.

The Prophet's own father, Abdallah, contracted a matrilineal marriage with Amina Bint Wahb.

> When Abdallah Ibn Abd al-Muttalib married Amina Bint Wahb, he stayed with her for three days. Such was the prevailing custom when the man decided to marry a woman who stayed among her own tribe.[13]

Amina evidently stayed with her own kin. When Abdallah died

on his way home to Mecca from a trip, Amina was seven months pregnant with the Prophet. The child stayed with his mother until her death. He was then six years old. Only after her death was he taken in charge by his father's kin.[14]

Women's independence from their husbands and their insistence on sexual self-determination seem to have been possible only because they were backed by their own people. This independence persisted even with the growing affirmation of patrilineal trends in the Arab society of Muhammad's time, when the principle of marriage by capture or purchase was gaining ground.[15]

Marriage by capture or purchase implies a structure of virilocal polygamy. This was a novel idea in the Prophet's time, as is evidenced by his own inconsistent attitude towards it. Although he himself married thirteen women, he adamantly opposed Ali, his son-in-law, when the latter decided to contract a second marriage and thus provide Fatima, the Prophet's favourite daughter (who was not particularly known for her beauty), with an unwelcome co-wife.

> I will not allow Ali Ibn Abi Talib and I repeat, I will not allow Ali to marry another woman except if he divorces my daughter. She is a part of me, and what harms her, harms me.[16]

The Prophet appears to have known that it was harmful for a woman to share a husband. Another illustration is provided by the Ansar, the Prophet's political supporters. They thought polygamy so degrading that they urged one of their daughters, Leila Bint al-Khatim, not to marry the Prophet.[17] They argued that she was too proud. She might get jealous and make trouble in the household of the Prophet and thus provoke tension between him and his allies. A third example is that of the Prophet's wife (or concubine) Rayhana, whom he is supposed to have divorced because she was too jealous to bear sharing him with her co-wives. He remarried her when she regained control over her feelings.[18] But probably the most outstanding instance of rebellion against polygamy is that of Amina, the Prophet's great-granddaughter. Whenever she contracted a marriage, she insisted on keeping total control. Before marrying Zaid Ibn Umar she set these conditions: 'He will not touch another woman. He will not prevent her from spending his money, and will not oppose any decision she might make. Otherwise she will leave him.'[19]

Women's Resistance to Islam

Amina recognized that women were much happier before the Prophet's time. When asked why she was so funny and humorous and her sister, Fatima, so deadly serious, she answered

> It is because she [Fatima] was named after her Muslim grandmother [Fatima is the daughter of the Prophet] while I was named after my pagan great-great-grandmother, who died before Islam's arrival. [Amina is the mother of the Prophet.][20]

This idea is corroborated by historical incidents, some violent and bloody like the case of the so-called harlots of Hadramaut, others more peaceful like the insistence of early Muslim women on their freedom of action in initiating and ending sexual unions.

After the death of the Prophet in June 632, a broad movement of apostasy swept the Arabian peninsula, and the tribes refused to pay taxes to the Prophet's successor, the first caliph, Abu Bakr.[21] The movement was severely repressed and ended one year later, after fierce battles between Islam and its opponents. One of the movements of apostasy was led by a group of women who celebrated the death of the Prophet in a joyful atmosphere. The event is recorded in Ibn Habib al-Baghdadi's *Kitab al-Muhabbar*.[22]

> There were in Hadramaut six women, of Kinda and Hadramaut, who desired the death of the Prophet of God; they therefore [on hearing the news] dyed their hands with henna and played on the tambourine. To them came out the harlots of Hadramaut and did likewise so that some twenty-odd women joined the six.[23]

The caliph received two letters relating the event and asking him to punish the blasphemous women. Both letters were written by men. The caliph's answer to the governor of Kinda, ordering him to retaliate, reads as follows

> In the name of God, the compassionate, the merciful. From Abu Bakr to al-Muhajir Ibn Abi Umayyah. The two right-eous servants [of God] who remained steadfast in their religion when the greater part of their tribes apostasized (may God grant them the reward of the righteous for this and smite the others with the fate of the wicked) have written to me declaring that before them there are certain women of the people of Yemen who have desired the death of the Prophet of God, and that these have been joined by singing-girls of Kinda and prostitutes of Hadra-maut, and they have dyed their hands and shown joy and played on the tambourine in defiance of God and in contempt of His rights and those of His Prophet. When my letter reaches you, go to them with your horses and men, and strike off their hands. If anyone defends them against you, or stands between them and you, expostulate with him, telling him the enormity of the sin and enmity which he is committing; and if he repents, accept his repentance, but if he declines, break off negotiations with him and proceed to hostilities—God will not guide the traitors! However, I think, nay I am sure, that no man will condone the evil acts of these women or hinder you from smiting them away from the religion of Muhammad as one might smite off the wings of a gnat.[24]

If we interpret this opposition between a group of women and Islam as a clash of interests, we have to analyse what interests were at stake. First we must identify the parties. The identity of the first caliph is indisputable, but that of the women is not. The Muslim document dismisses them sum-marily as harlots. But this 'harlotry' was unusual indeed. The Muslim historian Ibn Habib al-Baghdadi identifies twelve of them. Two were grandmothers, one a mother, and seven were young girls. Three of the twelve belonged to the *ashraf* ('the noble class') and four to the tribe of Kinda, a royal tribe which provided Yemen with its kings.[25] Some of the men who intervened to defend the women against the Muslim governor's forces were from this same royal tribe. What kind of harlotry is practised by elderly grandmothers, young girls, the most noble of women, the members of princely houses? And why, in any case, was the clapping of tambourines by twenty-six women in the faraway villages of south Arabia so threatening to the powerful Muslim military order?

A.F.L. Beeston explains the conflict between the women and Islam as a clash between the old religion and the new.[26] He speculates that the new religion deprived these women dissidents of their position as pagan priestesses of the old temples, where religious prostitution was practised. This speculation is not altogether warranted by the text.

The text, however, does make two things clear. First, some women opposed Islam because it jeopardized their position. Whatever that position was, it was evidently more advantageous than the one Islam granted them. Second, the opposition between these women and Islam was clearly grounded in the sexual field. The fact that the caliph labelled his opponents as harlots implies that Islam condemned their sexual practices, whatever they were, as harlotry. I believe that the incident of the harlots of Hadramaut is an example of Islam's opposition to prevailing sexual practices in pre-Islamic Arabia.

Matrilineal Trends in Pre-Muslim Society

Robertson Smith pointed to the sixth and seventh centuries as a transitional phase in Arab kinship history. He argued that the period of Islam's appearance had a multiplicity of sexual unions belonging to two trends: a matrilineal trend, which he calls *sadiqa* marrriage,[27] and a patrilineal trend he calls *ba'al* or dominion marriage.[28] The two systems, which existed side by side down to the Prophet's time,[29] were diametrically opposed to each other. Not only were they governed by different kinship laws, but they 'imply fundamental differences in the position of women and so in the whole structure of social relations'.[30] The difference between the two systems can be summarized as

	Matrilineal Trend	*Patrilineal Trend*
Kinship rule	Child belonged to the mother's group	Child belonged to the father's group
Paternity rule	Physical paternity unimportant: the genitor does not have rights over his offspring	Physical paternity important because the genitor must be the social father
Sexual freedom of women	Extended, her chastity has no social function	Limited, her chastity is a prerequisite for the establishment of the child's legitimacy
Status of women	Depends on her tribe for protection and food	Depends on her husband for protection and food
Geographical setting of marriage	Uxorilocal	Virilocal

Sadiqa marriage (from *sadiq*, 'friend', and *sadiqa*, 'female friend') is a union whose offspring belong to the woman's tribe. It is initiated by a mutual agreement between a woman and a man and takes place at the house of the woman, who retains the right to dismiss the husband. In *ba'al* marriage the offspring belong to the husband. He has the status of father as well as of his wife's *ba'al*, or 'lord', 'owner'. In such a marriage

> The wife, who follows her husband and bears his children, who are of his blood, loses the right freely to dispose of her person. Her husband has authority over her and he alone has the right of divorce.[31]

Robertson Smith concludes that Islam accelerated the transition from matriliny to patriliny by enforcing a marriage institution that had much in common with the patrilineal dominion marriage, and by condemning all matrilineal unions as *zina*.

Certainly Mecca made no exception to the rule that Arabian *ba'al* marriage was regarded as constituted by capture or by purchase, that the marital rights of the husband were a dominion over his wife, and that the disposal of her hand did not belong to the woman herself but to her guardian. For all this is still true even under Islam; the theory of Muslim law is still that marriage is purchase, and the party from whom the husband buys is the father, though by a humane illogicality the price becomes the property of the woman, and the husband's rights are not transferable. And so, though Islam softened some of the harshest features of the old law, it yet has set a permanent seal of subjection on the female sex by stereotyping a system of marriage which, at bottom, is nothing else than the old marriage of dominion.[32]

Sadiqa marriage was characterized by sexual freedom for women, symbolized by their sovereignty over the marital household, namely the tent in which they received their husbands.

> The women in *jahiliya*, or some of them, had the right to dismiss their husbands, and the form of dismissal was this: if they lived in a tent, they turned it around so that if the door faced east, it now faced west, and when the man saw this, he knew that he was dismissed, and he did not enter.[33]

It is evident that this kind of marriage could only be uxorilocal, since the woman remained with her tribe and depended on it. The symbolic gesture of dismissal was known as 'she draws a curtain between the husband and herself' and was used in the case of Muhammad Ibn Bashir, whose wife 'drew a curtain between him and her and disappeared'.[34]

The variety of sexual unions practised in pre-Islamic Arabia is best described by the reliable Muslim traditionalist Bukhari:

> Ibn Shihab said, Urwah Ibn al-Zubair informed him that Aisha, the wife of the Prophet (God bless and preserve him) informed him that marriage in *jahiliyah* was of four types:

1. *One was marriage of people as it is today*, where a man betroths his ward or his daughter to another man, and the latter assigns a dowry [bride price] to her and then marries her.

2. *Another type was where a man said to his wife when she was purified from her menses, send to N. and ask to have intercourse with him*; her husband then stays away from her and does not touch her at all until it is clear that she is pregnant from that [other] man with whom she sought intercourse. When it is clear that she is pregnant, her husband has intercourse with her if he wants. He acts thus simply from the desire for a child. This type of marriage was known as Nikah al-Istibda ['the marriage of seeking intercourse'].

3. *Another type was where a group of less than ten men used to visit the same woman* and all of them to have intercourse with her. If she became pregnant and bore a child, when some nights had passed after the birth she could send for them, and not a man of them might refuse. When they had come together in her presence, she would say to them, 'You [plural] know the result of your acts. I have borne a child and he is your [singular] child, N.' naming whoever she will by his name; her child is attached to him and the man may not refuse.

4 *The fourth type is where many men frequent a woman*, and she does not keep herself from any who comes to her. These women are the *baghaya* [prostitutes]. They used to set up at their doors banners forming a sign. Whoever wanted them went in to them. If one of them conceived and bore a child, they gathered together to her and summoned the physiognomists to designate as father the man whom the child resembled most. Then the child remained attached to him and was called his son, no objection to this course being possible. When Muhammad (God bless and preserve him) came preaching the truth, he destroyed all the types of marriage of the *jahiliyah* except that which people practise today [numbers added].[35]

The general picture that emerges from Bukhari's description is a system characterized by the coexistence of a variety of marriages, or rather sexual unions. In three of the four kinds of marriages, biological paternity seems unimportant and the concept of female chastity is therefore absent (2, 3, and 4). Two of the marriages were polyandrous, the woman having as many 'husbands' as she desired (3 and 4).

Another kind of marriage mentioned elsewhere by Bukhari is *mut'a* ('marriage of pleasure, or temporary marriage').

> If a man and a woman agree to live together, their partnership lasts three nights and if they want to extend it, they extend it, and if they decide to part, they part.[36]

Tarmidi gives a description of the practicality of such a union.

> In early Islam, when a man would arrive in a new town where he did not know anybody, he would marry a woman in exchange for a sum of money according to the length of the period of his stay, and she would keep his belongings and take care of him. This was practised until the verse forbidding it was revealed.[37]

Its sexual goal is affirmed in another traditionist's description. Imam Muslim writes.

> *Mut'a* . . . was a temporary marriage. The man would say to the woman, 'I will enjoy you for a certain period of time in exchange for a certain sum of money.' It was named *mut'a* [pleasure] because its main purpose was exclusively sexual pleasure, i.e., without procreation and other purposes usually expected from marriage. *Mut'a* was outlawed by the Book and the Sunna.[38]

It was practised in early Islam and is still practised by Muslims who follow the *Shia* trend.[39]

Compared to orthodox Muslim marriage, *mut'a* violates two fundamental principles of Islam's ideal of sexual union. First, its temporary and personal character gives the woman as much freedom as the man, in both the initiation and the termination of the marriage. Muslim marriage reserves these rights to the man only, subordinates the woman's consent to that of her guardian, and alienates her freedom to divorce by subordinating it to a judge's decision. Second, such a union implies different paternity rules than the ones on which Muslim marriage is based, the rule according to which the social father must be the biological genitor. For Robertson Smith

> *Mut'a* in short is simply the last remains of that type of marriage which corresponds to a law of mother-kinship, and Islam condemns it and makes it 'the sister of harlotry' because it does not give the husband a legitimate offspring, i.e. an offspring that is reckoned to his own tribe and has right of inheritance within it.[40]

The panorama of female sexual rights in pre-Islamic culture reveals that women's sexuality was not bound by the concept of legitimacy. Children belonged to their mother's tribe. Women had sexual freedom to enter into and break off unions with more than one man, either simultaneously or successively. A woman could either reserve herself to one man at a time, on a more or less temporary basis, as in *mut'a* marriage, or she could be visited by many husbands at different times whenever their nomadic tribe or trade caravan came through the woman's town or camping ground.[41] The husband would come and go; the main unit was the mother and child within an entourage of kinfolk.[42]

The linguistic legacy of the matrilineal past has survived in Arabic. The word *rahim*, meaning 'womb', is 'the most general word for kinship'.[43] *Batn* ('belly') is the technical term for a clan or sub-tribe.[44] The word *umm* ('mother') is the origin of *umma* ('community' in general and, after Islam, the Muslim community). According to Salama Musa, the fact that the word *haya*, 'life', is also a name for the female reproductive apparatus expresses the old Arab belief that women had the gift of giving life while the male's role was 'pure sexual pleasure'.[45]

Robertson Smith copiously documents the shift from patrilineal to matrilineal marriage with examples from both Muslim and pre-Islamic sources.[46]

The Effects of Muslim Marriage on Pre-Muslim Society

If we consider marriage as a 'rearrangement of social structure' and social structure as 'any arrangement of persons in institutionalized relationships',[47] then a change in the marriage system would imply far-reaching socio-economic changes. A change in kinship implies a dislocation of old socio-economic structures, and the appearance of new networks based on new units. In *Muhammad at Mecca* and *Muhammad at Medina*,[48] Montgomery Watt analyses Arabia's socio-economic foundations in the transitional period during the sixth and early seventh centuries. He attributes Islam's sweeping success among the tribes (Muhammad started preaching in 613, and when he died in 632 most of Arabia's tribes were already converted) to a pre-existing malaise caused by the disintegration of the tribal system. Insecurity and discontent were spreading because of the rise of a thriving mercantile economy which was corroding traditional tribal communalism. Individuals engaged in trading were motivated by new mercantile allegiances which often clashed with traditional tribal ones.[49] In thriving urban settlements like Mecca, the contradictions between new and old allegiances were particularly acute. The violation of traditional allegiances brought about isolation and economic insecurity among the weakest members of the tribe. Responsible members who were supposed to administer property for the communal good were now lured by individualistic pursuits and neglected their traditional role as protectors of the weak.[50] Women and children were among those most directly affected by the disruption of the old networks of solidarity since they had no institutionalized access to property through inheritance.[51] Inheritance was the privilege of those who took part in battles and acquired booty: able-bodied adult males.

But if women did not have the right to inherit, that does not mean that they had no access to goods, as some Muslim writers believe.[52] Their protection and economic well-being were the core of a tribe's prestige and the embodiment of its honour.[53] It has been argued that many of Islam's institutions were a response to the new needs that emerged with the disintegration of tribal communalism, a means of absorbing the insecurity generated by such disintegration. Polygamy, for example, has been described as such an institution.[54] The Prophet, concerned about the fate of women who were divorced, widowed or unmarried orphans, decided to create a kind of responsibility system whereby unattached women were resituated in a family unit in which a man could protect them, not just as kinsman but as husband. The fact that polygamy was instituted by the Koran after the disaster of Uhud, a battle in which many Muslim males were slain, substantiates this theory.[55]

Moreover, the Prophet had a vested interest in reintegrating women, made helpless by the breakdown of tribal solidarity, into new solidarity units, because otherwise they were likely to seek protection in transitory sexual unions considered as *zina* by Islam. It is here that one sees the genius of Islam. That its institutions were appreciated is shown by its success in connecting both communal and self-serving tendencies and channelling these otherwise contradictory trends into the most cohesive social order Arabia has ever known. The communal tendencies were channelled into warfare for *Pax Islamica*, and the self-serving tendencies were mainly vented in the institution of the family, which allowed new allegiances and new ways to transfer private possession of goods while simultaneously providing tight controls over women's sexual freedom.

Watt suggests that the *umma* resembled the tribe in many of its premisses. The responsibility system within the *umma* was very similar to the tribal principles of blood-feud and *lex talionis*: 'For the military prestige of the *umma*, it was essential in Arabian conditions that a Muslim should never go unavenged.'[56]

But the *umma* steered the tribes' bellicosity, usually invested in tribal feuding, in a new direction—the holy war.[57] The old allegiance to the tribe was replaced by an allegiance entirely different in both form and content. The new form is the *umma* and the basic unit is not the tribe, but the individual. The bond between individuals is not kinship but a more abstract concept, communion in the same religious belief.

In less than a few decades, the razzia-inclined nomadic tribes, which were a great obstacle to Arabia's thriving trade routes and centres, were persuaded to give in to the *umma*, which required unconditional surrender to the will of Allah. Consequently, their quest for booty was deflected from internal attacks and channelled into holy war against the common enemy. The wealthy Byzantine and Persian empires fell to the Arabs before they were even fully aware of the existence of Islam. (Persia was conquered in 642, twenty years after the *hijra*; the first siege of Constantinople took place in 670.)

Parallel to the harnessing of tribal bellicosity in the service of the Muslim community, there was a similar absorption of self-serving tendencies into the family structure. One of these channelling mechanisms was the concept of fatherhood and legitimacy, which allowed full expression to the believers' self-interest.

> It would be natural for him [any man in an increasingly patrilineal society] at the same time to become specially interested in his own children and to want them to succeed to the wealth he had appropriated. In a matrilineal family, the control of the family property would normally pass from a man to his sister's son.[58]

For a man to transfer his goods to his sons implies that he has sons, which had not generally been clear. Biological paternity had been considered unimportant in the pre-existing systems, and the patterns of female sexuality made it difficult to establish who had begotten whom. Islam dealt with this obstacle in two ways. As we have seen, it outlawed most previous sexual practices as *zina* and institutionalized strict control over paternity in the form of the *idda*, or waiting period. The *idda* can be seen as the best proof both of the previous disregard for biological paternity and of Islamic curtailment of female sexual rights, since no equivalent period was instituted for men.

As the institution of the *idda* shows, obsession with depriving a woman of her power to determine paternity is difficult to satisfy without her cooperation. The *idda* implies that the Muslim God does not expect a woman's cooperation, although He explicitly requires it as a condition of her oath of allegiance. Verse 228 of the second sura declares

> It is not lawful for them [women] that they should conceal
> that which Allah hath created in their wombs, if they are
> believers in Allah . . .

The fact that despite His unequivocal orders to women, Allah decided to check on them by institutionalizing the waiting period shows that He did not expect them to obey the divine order. The expectation that women will not cooperate, that they will need to be coerced, explains man's religious duty to control the women under his roof. The man is responsible not only for satisfying the woman sexually and providing for her economically, but, as a policeman of the Muslim order, also for disciplining and guarding his female relatives.

Watt noted that the idea of a police force distinct from the community was unknown among the Arabs.[59] A rigid code of honour compelled every individual to tailor his actions, which were entirely involved in communal pursuit, to the community's standards. In Islam the same mechanism operated, but the man's burden was heavier because the *umma* conceded him an individual territory of which he would be the master and for which he would be held responsible: 'The man is the guardian of his family and he is responsible . . .'[60]

Conclusion

The social order created by the Prophet, a patrilineal mono-theistic state, could exist only if the tribe and its allegiances gave way to the *umma*. The Prophet found the institution of the family a much more suitable unit of socialization than the tribe. He saw the tightly controlled patriarchal family as necessary to the creation of the *umma*.

The Prophet's religious vision, his personal experiences, and the structure of the society he was reacting against all contributed to the form Islamic society took. The assumptions behind the Muslim social structure—male dominance, the fear of *fitna*, the need for sexual satisfaction, the need for men to love Allah above all else—were embodied in specific laws which have regulated male-female relations in Muslim countries for fourteen centuries.

Today, however, with modernization, basic changes are occurring not only in economic structures but in social relations as well, and these challenge the underlying principles of Islam as a social order. If we define modernization as involving, among other things, the integration of the economies of the Arab-Muslim countries into the world market, with all that this process entails in disintegration, upheaval, conflict, and contradiction, then we may say that one of the areas in which this integration is having decisive effects is home life, the structure of family relations, and especially the dynamic of relations between the sexes.

The Arab-Muslim economies have already gone far along the road to integration into the world market. In his book *The Arab Economy Today* Samir Amin shows that 'the Arab world occupies a very special place in the Third World as a whole and is the part of it most closely integrated into the contemporary world system'.[61] This economic integration has been accompanied by an ideological integration that is far less widely accepted. An Arab man buys an automobile produced by French, Swedish, or American factories and he considers it his property for which he has paid a certain price. The same man has a far more ambiguous attitude towards the import of what might be called symbolic capital. The great struggles in the Arab world today concern this attitude towards Western symbolic capital, in particular the fight for authenticity (*al-asala*), which now figures prominently in all current debates, whether these be political, social, or economic.

One of the areas in which the import of Western symbolic capital (ideas) has been evident is social relations, especially liberal concepts like human rights, civil law, and the structure of relational models. Concepts like political party, trade union, parliament are among the ideological exports of former colonial countries of Europe to the formerly colonized Arab societies. In fact, the Arab nationalist movement itself may be regarded as a strange Trojan Horse within which the transfer of ideas took place in a context of violently anti-Western, xenophobic struggle.

The fact is that economic dependence (the transfer of machinery, for instance) seems not to have elicited among contemporary

Arab leaders the same virtually neurotic reactions as have been aroused by the transfer of symbolic capital, by the ideological dependence that seems directly and openly to challenge the key notion of identity.

If the debate is wide-ranging, the stakes are high. What is of most interest to us here is the transfer, during the twentieth century, of ideas from liberal capitalist Europe to the Muslim societies, especially the elements of Western democracy generally grouped under the label 'human rights', which have been the subject of international treaties some of which directly concern relations between the sexes. The fact that the Arab countries have manifested their resistance to this transfer of liberal ideas about relations between the sexes by refusing to sign certain international treaties and conventions has not prevented them from ratifying many others that are clearly prejudicial to the central principle of the Muslim family: male supremacy and the systematic inhibition of feminine initiative, of female self-determination. This is the pertinent point in understanding the new trends in relations between the sexes.

For instance, to understand the virtually hysterical attitude of Arab-Muslim leaders to the emergence of female self-determination which is inherent in the economic and political changes these countries are now experiencing, we must place this attitude in its historic and cultural context, which is to say in the 'Muslim time-frame' according to which the year 622 marks the birth of civilization and the year 621 is still a time of the chaos of ignorance, of *jahiliya*. Female self-determination, feminine initiative, whether in the home or the outside world, is the very embodiment of the absence of order, the absence of Muslim laws. Hence the importance of looking back at the roots, at the pre-Islamic period, if we are to comprehend some of the behaviour patterns and cultural attitudes of the Arab world today.

In analysing the condition of women in the Muslim countries, it must never be forgotten that ideologically the year 622 still lives in the formulation of future strategies. The time scales of contemporary Muslim societies are very special: fourteen centuries seem to have elapsed without major upheavals or fatal discontinuity, and the future promises to be a continuation of the past. The emergence of feminine initiative consequent to such unremarkable features of present-day economies as the individual wage is reminiscent in the collective memory of the conflicts of *jahiliya*, re-issued and projected forward as the shape of the future.

In modern Muslim societies women who seek university degrees and jobs and who invest a large part of their energies in strictly individualist aspirations conjure up, in a whole inventory of symbolic images, the ghosts of women of the pre-Islamic Arab aristocracy, ghosts that have never been definitively buried. Islam's trenchant opposition to *jahiliya* has paradoxically made *jahiliya* a fundamental matrix of the Muslim psyche. And that psyche, through a strange regressive reflex, sees the advent of the industrial era, the era of individual wages and individual votes, as heralding a new *jahiliya*. Women—with their demands for initiative and self-determination—are a symbolically potent component of both the old *jahiliya* and the new, the one that opens with the modern era.

PART TWO

Anomic Effects of Modernization
on Male-Female Dynamics

4
The Modern Situation:
Moroccan Data

I have outlined a theoretical model of the traditional Muslim concept of female sexuality based on Ghazali's ideas of Muslim marriage. I now would like to use his description of the Muslim family not to evaluate the historical changes in that family, but to understand the present situation by contrasting it with an ideal type. I will compare Ghazali's ideal family with Moroccan reality as revealed by the data I have collected, in order to illustrate the trends shaping modern male-female dynamics.

I collected my data in Morocco during the summer of 1971. At first my main concern was how to go about investigating the changes occurring in male-female relations. I casually asked about fifty people (roughly half males and half females), 'What do you think is the main change that has taken place in the family and in women's situation in the last decades?'

Almost everyone I interviewed mentioned, at one point or another, sexual desegregation. The idea was presented in different ways: 'women used to be protected', 'women didn't use to go everywhere', 'women used to stay at home', 'there used to be more order, women were strictly controlled'. But the underlying idea was always the same. So I decided to concentrate on the dimension of male-female dynamics in which the changes seem to have been particularly noticeable—the use of space by the sexes.

I wanted to get two kinds of data, some describing family life in both traditional and modern settings (where the wife holds a job outside the home or has free access to the outside world) and some describing the present tensions in Moroccan society relating to sexual interaction. I opted for lengthy interviews with women to get the first kind of data. For the second, I used letters from a religious counselling service on Moroccan state television which receives hundreds of letters every day from citizens with problems. I was allowed to borrow 402 of these letters.

The Interviews With Women

Because of the theoretical nature of my research and the scope of what I wanted to investigate—sexual desegregation—I decided to limit my field of observation as much as possible. I selected data concerning one numerically tiny stratum of the Moroccan population: the urban petty-bourgeoisie. Despite its size, this grouping has played an important political role in other Arab-Muslim societies and is likely to do the same in Morocco.

I conducted about a hundred interviews, lasting twenty to thirty minutes each, with women selected according to categories pertinent to my research (traditional women, modern women), before proceeding to in-depth interviews. These, conducted during the summer of 1971, lasted between two and six hours each and required between two and six sessions depending on circumstances (presence of in-laws, noise level, mood of the person being interviewed, presence of adult women able to look after small children during the interview, etc.). The categories 'modern' and 'traditional' cover a range of differences in age, education, employment, and so on. Tables 1 and 2 below (see p. 92) list some differences between traditional and modern women and supply the age and marital status of the fourteen women with whom I conducted in-depth interviews; the jobs of the modern women and of the men supporting the traditional women are also given.

In order to examine the trends of modernization more closely I tried to interview mothers (traditional) with their daughters (modern). I succeeded only four times in realizing this combination. The women concerned are indicated in the tables by the same last initial. The interviews were non-directed and lengthy, conducted in the normal rhythm of a 'gossip' exchange.

I concentrated on just a few interviews as sources for quotation in order to increase readers' familiarity with the individuals described. Within each chapter I used information from one interview as much as possible. For example, the interviewee coded Fatiha F. was the main source for the mothers-in-law and not only because Fatiha is a wonderful conversationalist— also because the contradictions of the relation mother-son-wife reached almost archetypal dimensions in her case.

A systematic reading of (or rather listening to) the tapes of the interviews revealed two major differences between the lives of traditional and modern women. For the traditional women sexual segregation had been very strict all their lives. For the modern women sexual segregation had been strict only during puberty, when they were made aware of the importance of their behaviour to the family honour. The modern women did not feel that sexual segregation was an important factor in their lives now.

The other major difference between the traditional and modern women was their perception of who was the most important person in their daily lives, which person they had the most intense relationship with. For the traditional women it was their mother-in-law. For the modern women it was their husband.

That these are the major differences suggests a link between the institution of sexual segregation and the important role in the family traditionally accorded the husband's mother. But I had no clue as to the nature of the link until I had done a content analysis of the letters to the counselling service.

The Counselling Letters

The four hundred letters analysed are a sample of the thousands sent to a counselling service financed and run by the government. It is broadcast daily on the national network, which has, besides entertainment programmes, many community-oriented projects. For example, divorces pronounced by judges on grounds of desertion are announced on the radio, thereby disseminating news to a large number of illiterate Moroccans who would otherwise not have access to this information.

Information on Women Interviewed

Table 1

	Traditional Women	*Modern Women*
Literacy	Illiterate	Literate
Job	Work within the home	Work outside the home
Sexual Segregation	Very strict	Very loose
Marriage	Arranged by the parents	Woman chose own partner
Age	Born before World War II	Born after World War II (when the nationalists' influence opened up schools for girls)

Table 2

Traditional Women

	Marital Status	*Age*	*Occupation of the Male Supporting Her*
Halima H.	Widowed	60	Son—Civil Servant
Hayat H.	Married	40	Husband—Civil Servant
Fatiha F.	Married	45	Husband—Civil Servant
Kenza	Married	50	Husband—Retired Civil Servant
Tamou T.	Widowed	48	Brother—Teacher
Khata	Married	48	Husband—Works in electric company
Salama	Widowed	60	Son—Agricultural Technician
Maria M.	Repudiated	55	Son—Army Officer

Modern Women

	Marital Status	*Age*	*Her Occupation*
Faiza F.	Married	22	Laboratory Assistant
Mona M.	Married	26	Teacher
Tahra T.	Single	25	Medical Student (works part-time and has grant)
Tama	Repudiated	30	Public Relations Officer
Lamia	Repudiated	30	Accountant
Safia	Single	25	Secretary

Counselling has always been important in Muslim life because of the freedom accorded to the individual. There is no clergy, no institutionalized intermediary between the individual and God. Every sensible adult is responsible for his thoughts and deeds. To be a decent believer requires more than anything else the intention to be so—that is, the intention to subordinate one's acts to the divine law. Whenever the individual doubts his knowledge of divine law, he is supposed to seek guidance from people trained in the matter. The Qadi Moulay Mustapha Alaoui, whose services are free of charge and delivered by radio, is probably the most popular counsellor in the country. He usually groups letters by subject and tries to answer one specific theme each day. The themes emerging in the letters determined their codification and content analysis.

Because of the Arabic formula that heads most letters—'From Mr. or Mrs. so and so, from the town of so and so'—the sex and residence of the letter-writers were usually identifiable. The letters also frequently mention age and marital status. An analysis of the sex, geographical distribution, marital status, and age of the letter-writers appears in Table 3 (see page 95). Whenever the handwriting was too difficult to decipher or the information was lacking, the letter was coded blank.

The coding for the content analysis was suggested by the themes that emerged from the letters. The majority dealt with problems relating to the family. The way I coded the content of the letters is illustrated by some examples of the variables I listed under the heading 'Pre-Marital Tensions'.

Variable 9: The youth's decision to marry
  1. Falling in love
  2. Wanting to marry the person of one's choice
  3. Combination of 1 and 2.

Variable 10: The parents' stand
  1. Parents interfere in offspring's choice
  2. Parents openly oppose the offspring's choice
  3. Parents force the offspring to marry a person of the parents' choice
  4. Combination of 1 and 2
  5. Combination of 1 and 3.

Variable 14: Parents' response to children's marital plans
  1. Curse
  2. Threaten to curse
  3. Open conflict, son-family
  4. Open conflict, daughter-family.

As is evident from the kinds of themes I found, a controversial question in modern Morocco is who chooses the marital partner. Is it the youth or the parents? According to the letters, parents think it their right to choose their offspring's partner in marriage, and the offspring think it their right to choose for themselves. The traditional Muslim ideas about marriage are in direct conflict with the aspirations and desires of the young generations.

My data suggests, and I believe, that Islam's concepts of female sexuality and women's contribution to society (as I outlined them in Part One) still determine the primary features of the Muslim family. The role played by sexual segregation, arranged marriage, the mother's importance in her son's life, all seem to be part of a system that discourages heterosexual couple relations even within the conjugal unit.

Modernization, on the other hand, encourages desegregation, independent choice of marriage partner, and the mobility of the nuclear family. That this open clash of ideologies leads to confusion and anxiety is apparent both in the counselling letters and in the interviews with women.

My modest aim in this research is not to irritate the reader by claiming to have uncovered the *truth* about the new male-female dynamic that has emerged in modern Moroccan society. I leave truth to those who seek certainty. My own feeling is that we move forward faster and live better when we seek doubt. If I manage to induce readers to doubt their prejudices and stereotypes about relations between the sexes, then I will have succeeded beyond my hopes. The qualitative analysis is not intended to flood the reader with statistical truths, which are in any case at anyone's disposal at the offices of the census department in Rabat. No, qualitative analysis ought to have the opposite effect: not to fortify your certitudes but to destroy them. It is understandable that a good number of walking dead may not appreciate that.

Table 3

INFORMATION ABOUT
LETTER WRITERS

SEX
(indicated in 369 letters)

	Number	Percentage
Female Writers	160	43
Male Writers	209	57

GEOGRAPHICAL ORIGIN
(indicated in 298 letters)

	Number	Percentage
Writers from Big Cities	210	70
Writers from Elsewhere	88	30

MARITAL STATUS
(indicated in 175 letters)

Single	46
Widowed	4
Married	48
Marriage Broken (Unspecified)	2

AGE
(indicated in 107 letters)

Teenagers (Under 20)	45
Young Adults (Between 20 and 25)	39
Adults (Over 25)	8
Elderly (When the writers describe themselves thus)	8

Moreover, as a researcher, whether in the domain of theory or in the analysis of particular material, I claim the inalienable right to make mistakes. Just as readers have the right to disagree, to draw different conclusions. The objective is to arouse discussion about our behaviour toward the other sex, and about the political implications of that behaviour. By 'political' I do not mean the democratic infrastructure (how parliaments, parties, and trade unions, for example, allow for the spread of democracy); I have in mind rather the relations we establish with the people closest to us, with whom we share the greatest interests and weave the most intense and most intimate human relation possible—in other words, the people with whom we share domestic space. It is quite inconceivable for a human being who does not cherish democratic relations in a domain considered non-political, like the household (in which life's essential functions are enacted: eating, sleeping, love-making), to seek it in the high ground of democracy, the party cell or the parliamentary chamber.

It is essential that the nature of democratic male-female relations be clarified. This basic question concerns all of us and is particularly vital for me, a woman living in a Muslim society.

5
Sexual Anomie As Revealed by the Data

Relations between the sexes seem to be going through a period of anomie, of deep confusion and absence of norms. The traditional norms governing relations between the sexes are violated every day by a growing majority of people without their incurring legal or social sanctions. One such tradition is sexual segregation, the systematic prevention of interaction between men and women not related to each other by either marriage or blood. Sexual segregation divides all social space into male and female spaces.

The overlap between male and female areas is limited and regulated by a host of rituals. When a man invites a friend to share a meal at his house, he knocks on his own door and in a loud voice asks the women 'to make way' ('amlu triq). The women then run to hide in dark corners, leaving the courtyard free to be crossed by the stranger. The guest will remain with his host, seated in the men's room. If he needs to go to the toilet, the ritual of 'amlu triq is staged again, preventing the taboo situation of interaction between strangers of different sexes.

Similar rituals surround the trespassing of women into male spaces, which until recently was limited to a very few occasions such as a visit to a saint's tomb, to the public baths and to relatives at births, deaths and marriages. The veil is an expression of the invisibility of women on the street, a male space *par excellence*.

According to my interviews, sexual segregation was seen as a natural part of life by women in their fifties, but merely as an option for women now in their thirties. Women's right to traditionally male spaces is far more institutionalized or even accepted, whether at the level of laws or underlying ideology.

The anomie stems from the gap between ideology and reality, for more and more women are using traditionally male spaces, going without the veil, and determining their own lives. The anomie created by the fissures between ideology, belief, and practice is well illustrated in the following letter received by the religious counselling service.

Casabalanca, 18 May 1971   Letter 88
       To his highness, Professor Moulay Mustapha Alaoui
Sir,
    Nowadays the majority of people go to swim in the sea, they go to beaches during the summer months. Men, women, boys, and girls meet and mix together. They also mix with Christians and Jews, everyone looking at everybody else's nudity. Is this permissible in a Muslim society? I asked this question a long time ago. I did not hear your answer on the radio. Could it be that you did not receive it?

Desegregation intensifies the sexual component of hetero-sexual interactions, but society fails to provide any acceptable models for sexual interactions. The consequent doubts and anxieties are evident in the following letters.

Taza, 13 March 1971   Letter 46
       To the religious scholar Moulay Mustapha
Sir,
    I was in love with a young man. He asked me to let him kiss and caress me. I gave in to his demands. I was encouraged in doing so by a girlfriend, but we did not go as far as having intercourse. After a while I discovered that he was not serious about our relation and I kept away from him. And I promised myself that I would never commit such sinful practices again. Is what I have done permissible or forbidden by Islam? What can I do to erase such sin? Thank you! Thank you!

Rabat, 14 June 1971   Letter 100
        From Miss K . . . . . to his highness Pr. M.M.
I send you a perfumed salutation,
    Is it permissible for a young unmarried girl who is not
engaged to be kissed by a man who is not engaged to her
and does not intend to marry her? I will be very thankful if
you can answer my question with as many details as you
can. Many thanks, sir.

A content analysis of the 402 letters reveals that sexuality
(presented in terms of questions about love, marriage, deviant
practices, and so on) seems to be one of the preoccupations of
the letter-writers. The majority of the letters ask about the
permissibility or non-permissibility of sexual actions from the
religious point of view. Most of the questions are about acts—
like swimming 'nude' (a woman is 'nude' if she is not veiled) on
a mixed-sex beach or being kissed by someone other than the
legal husband—that are illicit and sinful according to tradition.
Interaction between the sexes, though increasing, is still an
unusual phenomenon in Moroccan society. Traditional, absolute
segregation between the sexes continues to pervade many parts
of the country.

Sexual Problems in Rural Areas

A survey of some rural areas[1] revealed that each village controls
its youth so closely that young men have no access to women
and engage in sexual practices considered deviant by their
society's standards. For example, of those who answered a
questionnaire:
    14% confessed practising masturbation or sodomy;
    20% practise homosexuality;
    34% go to a brothel in the nearest town as often as they can
afford it.[2]

    In the absence of thorough studies of the sexual practices of
Moroccan youth as a whole, we can draw no firm conclusions
about sexual problems in general. But it is clear that sexual

segregation is still a reality for rural youth.

Almost two-thirds of Morocco's fifteen million people live in rural areas,[3] and 56 percent of the total population are under twenty.[4] In the rural areas surveyed, 87 percent of the people were under twenty-one, and 78 percent of these youths dreamed of going to live in town. One of the reasons they gave for that preference was that women are available in towns.

> In town there are as many girls as you want.
> You can find brothels only in towns.
> In town women walk with heads uncovered, wearing short dresses; you can always take a chance with them.[5]

Sexual segregation is enforced in one village with a characteristically violent censure.

> If you try to leave the village with a girl who is more than twelve years old, more than thirty people will follow you. They start throwing stones and shouting at you. It is not like in town; you need to take so many precautions.[6]

Because of the restrictions on heterosexual encounters, the rural Moroccan male is brought to perceive women solely in terms of sexual need; both in and outside marriage women are merely a more suitable way of satisfying sexual needs than animals or other males.

> At the age of seventeen I became aware of what was going on. I left animals and friends [with whom he practised homosexuality] because I realized it was detrimental to my energy. I learned that one can find whores in the centre of B_____. When I don't have money I don't hesitate to steal something so that I can go about my business.[7]

Most young men are resentful of being forced into sexual practices they abhor. They dream of getting married, and do so as soon as they can find a job, which is rather difficult. Unemployment, which takes the form of under-employment in the countryside, often reaches dizzying proportions.[8] According to the 1971 census,[9] those suffering most from unemployment are from fifteen to twenty-four years old. When looking for a job for the first time, 83 percent of this group cannot find one.[10] The young men resent the fact that older men who have more money monopolize and marry most of the young girls.

> I fell in love with a girl in the village and she was aware of it. I didn't have any money. . . . . A civil servant [a man who has a job and comes from a more important urban centre] came along and took away the girl I loved. So, I will not hide this from you, I went back to animals again.[11]

In the most traditional rural society, there are no unmarried adolescent girls. A survey done by Malika Belghiti among the female rural population reveals that 50 percent of the girls are married before they reach puberty, and another 37 percent marry during the first two years following puberty.[12] One way rural society avoids the problem of sexual love between young people seems to be to have girls marry young.

According to my interviews, the ideal age for marriage in the traditional structure is thirteen. Early marriage is seen as a prestigious event in a woman's life. It implies that she was beautiful enough to be asked for early. Only ugly, unattractive girls marry late. Without exception, all the women interviewed said they married before having their first period and when asked to give a specific age they said thirteen. I had the chance to check on one of them. I asked a childhood friend of hers if she remembered when Mrs. F_____ got married.

> She lied to you! She was a very old girl when she got married. She was a problem for her family. Haven't you noticed that she is rather homely?
>
> (How old do you think she was when she got married?)
>
> I swear she must have been at least twenty! I wish I was there when you were interviewing her. She wouldn't have dared to indulge herself. And how could you believe it? No one will call her a beauty, and don't tell me it is old age! She was always as ugly as famine days.

In urban Morocco girls seem to marry much later. A family-planning survey conducted by the government in 1966[13] revealed that the ideal age of marriage for girls in towns is much later than puberty.

Ideal Age at Marriage	For Men	For Women
According to Men	23	17
According to Women	25	19

Young men in towns have a chance to seek adolescent women of their own age and think about marrying them, while in rural settings all the young girls belong to husbands already.

Sexual Problems in Urban Areas

Our data deals mainly with urban problems; 70 percent of the letters come from urban centres. They convey the idea that sexual segregation in the city is not as absolute as it is in rural areas: young men actually do have access to women, often older and/or married women.

Casablanca, 1971   Letter 89
I am a fifteen-year-old high-school student. Please guide me. Here is my problem: there is a married maid in our house. She cannot bear children; she is sterile. I used to be with her often and I used to visit her in her house and then I started sleeping with her. I mean, commiting *zina* with her. I did this many times. Please guide me. What can I do to redeem myself?

Casablanca, 16 January 1971   Letter 169
I am a twenty-year-old man. I am trapped by a problem that I cannot solve. In our neighbourhood lives a 35-year-old woman who has children but no husband. I made advances to her once and what was bound to happen happened. I am asking God for forgiveness. After that I kept away from her. Two years have passed since then and now I look at her differently, as if she was my mother or

my sister. In fact, our relation has evolved into a respectful, brotherly relation.

Now I am coming to the subject. This woman has a seventeen-year-old daughter who used to live with her grandmother and who has just come to stay with her mother. At the beginning I never paid much attention to her, but I noticed her kind manner towards me. I also noticed that she was very affectionate towards me. One day she confessed to me that she was in love with me and I responded to her affections. . . .

But I can't forget what happened between her mother and me and often I am torn between my love for her and the desire to flee from her. She is an ideal girl for me and I feel a lot of affection for her. Once she extracted from me the promise to marry her.[14] Moreover, my mother suggested her as a possible bride for me. I am trapped. There is no reason I should refuse. *Is this marriage possible, is it licit according to religious law?*[15]

But most of the letters reveal that young men in towns seek contact with girls of the same age, want to marry them, and when they succeed in getting engaged, go further than a kiss.

Casablanca, 17 May 1971   Letter 180
Sir,

I am twenty-three years old. I met a girl who is nineteen. I fell in love with her and went to her parents and asked her hand in marriage. We have had to wait for a while before getting married because I don't have enough money for that yet.

But one day our sexual desire overwhelmed us and, therefore, I deprived her of her treasure, of her 'honour'. This happened after we had written the marriage contract though. We don't want to tell her parents because we have not had the marriage ceremony yet. Does religious law forbid what we did? My bride is as anxious as I because she has to live with her parents until the ceremony can take place.

But not all young men are as lucky as he was. Their desire to marry girls of their own choosing brings strong opposition from their parents. Consequently, sexuality in urban centres often assumes the aspect of a generational conflict between parents and children. Twenty percent of the 402 letters centre on this conflict. They reveal the young people's inclinations, their parents' attitudes, and often how the conflict is resolved. An examination of these themes and other variables such as age, sex, and size of the town, gives interesting insight into the shape of the conflict.

Parental Opposition to Love Marriage

The conflict centres on the parents' customary right to arrange marriage, and the young people's rejection of this right and insistence upon their right to marry for love. The parents believe the choice of a sexual partner for their daughter or son is their decision. (Incidentally, this gives them tremendous power over their children's lives.) Young Moroccans claim that they should choose their own sexual partners. The younger the individual, the more likely he is to insist on his right to love as he chooses. Of the letters concerning this conflict, 70 percent are written by teenagers and 30 percent by individuals between twenty and twenty-five.

Agadir, June 1971   Letter 5
    From Mr._____

I am a 22-year-old man. I have a father; I lost my mother when I was a child. My father got married after my mother's death. I asked my maternal aunt's daughter to marry me in 1961. [Child engagements have disappeared in general but if there is a strong attraction between young people it is common for the young man to make it known so that no one can take his beloved cousin from him.] My father opposed this marriage, knowing how much I loved this girl. This year I decided to marry her during the summer holidays. My father has announced that he will not be present at my marriage and that he will do whatever he can to prevent it from taking place. He wants to force me to leave the girl I have loved for so many years in order to marry a girl of his choice whom I have never met but who happens to belong to my father's wife's family.

How can I solve such a problem? Can I marry the girl I love? What does the religious law say about a person of my age who marries without the father's approval? What does God say about this? My stepmother is the one who encourages my father to refuse my marriage.

Fez, 8 June 1971   Letter 6

I am employed as a clerk in a company. I have a father who lives in the country far from me. I met a girl I want to marry and I promised to marry her and she promised to marry me. I wrote to my father announcing the news, hoping that he would rejoice with me but he did not. He opposes the marriage. He wants me to marry a woman from the country. I cannot do that because I cannot conceive of my life without this girl anymore and if I try to part from her I might find myself in a situation which is dangerous not only for me but for the Muslim *umma* as well, and for the Muslim religion too.

Please advise me about what is best for us and our religion.

The love protest voiced by young men is echoed by young women. The most fanatical advocates of the couple's rights, they write 70 percent of the letters about love.

Letter 7

From Miss_____

I am fifteen years old. A man came and asked for my hand from my parents. He has a bad temper and bad manners. He likes forbidden things like smoking, but kif. [Smoking kif, or hashish, despite what Western tourists think, is considered a shameful addiction.] And of course my parents gave me to him. I have not accepted the marriage and I am not going to. But the problem is that when the contract is about to be written by the justice officer [remember, it is a guardian who gives the girl in marriage], they do not intend to let me know. They intend to take another girl and write a fake contract. Then I will be sacrificed. My last decision if they write the contract is definite: I will commit suicide to free myself from these oppressive people. What does the religious law say concerning parents who fake their daughter's marriage? I prefer to kill myself whatever the law says.

Nonetheless, while 80 percent of the boys express their intention to marry their beloved, only 20 percent of the girls dare to go as far as that. This is probably because Moroccan girls, however 'modern' they may be, agree with their grandmothers, that it is the man who should ask for the girl's hand and not the other way around. This attitude seems wise and realistic given the fact that according to Moroccan law a woman cannot give herself in marriage: a male guardian has to do that.

The fact that girls do not initiate marriage is probably also the reason why there is a very low percentage of conflicts between parents and daughters as compared with conflicts between parents and sons. Of fourteen cases in which the conflict between parents and offspring had reached a crisis, ten involved the parents' opposition to the son's projected marriage.

The main weapon parents use against children seems to be the curse, parents being invested with Allah's power to curse or bless their children.[16] The potential destructiveness of the parents' curse is dramatized by the traditional fear expressed in sayings and proverbs. One of the most common is:

Who is cursed by parents cannot be saved by saints,
Who is cursed by saints can be saved by parents.

Persons cursed by their parents are likely to fail in whatever they attempt: their marriage will break up; their house will burn; their business enterprise will go bankrupt. In sum, a dreadful fate is to be expected on earth while waiting for hell in the next world. Consequently, parental opposition to children's marital projects is generally quite effective. Some young people say they feel resentment towards having to choose between their parents' blessings and their lover; some say they feel rebellious towards their parents but are afraid to act and feel paralysed; some plan to go ahead and act against their parents' will; finally, some threaten such drastic actions as breaking off relations with their parents or even committing suicide.

Why is Moroccan society, in the form of parental authority, reacting so negatively to the young people's desire for marriages based on love? Does conjugal love constitute an attack on Islam's attempt to integrate sexuality into society by subordinating the woman to the authority of her husband and outlawing love between them?

One feature of the sexual patterns that emerged from both the findings on the rural population and my own data on the urban population is that the heterosexual relationship is certainly the locus of change and conflict. Society seems to have a systematically negative attitude towards heterosexual love. In rural areas young people are prevented from forming any heterosexual relationships at all. In urban areas they are prevented from forming any permanent heterosexual relationships based on love.

In rural Morocco young men's access to young women is subject to strict and apparently effective control.[17] In urban centres access seems to be much less restricted. Young people meet frequently enough to fall in love and want to get married. Does this mean that sexual segregation is breaking down in urban areas?

I believe that sexual segregation, one of the main pillars of Islam's social control over sexuality, is breaking down. And it appears to me that the breakdown of sexual segregation permits the emergence of what the Muslim order condemns as a deadly enemy of civilization: love between men and women in general, and between husband and wife in particular.

6
Husband and Wife

The dynamics of shared spaces between the sexes can best be understood by analysing the functioning of the conjugal unit, the only model of heterosexual relationships that Muslim Moroccan society offers its children.

The ideal wife for the believer, according to Ghazali, is

> Beautiful, non-temperamental, with black pupils, and long hair, big eyes, white skin, and in love with her husband, looking at no one but him.[1]

Ghazali explains that Arabic has a word, *aruba*,[2] meaning a woman in love with her husband who feels like making love with him. This is one of the words used to describe the women promised to believers in Paradise.[3] He adds that the Prophet said that a woman who loves and obeys her husband is a gift from Allah. Such a woman would indeed be a miracle, given the conflict structure of the conjugal unit, based on a relationship of forces in which the most likely outcome is the woman's dislike of and rebellion against her husband.

Marriage as Conflict

All the women interviewed talked about *l'entente conjugale* as a magic phenomenon that levels all obstacles.

> When there is an *entente* between husband and wife, all obstacles can be overcome. Big crises become easy to deal with. When there is no *entente*, everything becomes a crisis.
>
> Fatiha F.

We never fought each other. He always treated me as a guest, with a lot of respect; he will do things before I express the need for them. For example, the day I decide to clean the house thoroughly I will try, on my own, to move the sofas and the wooden boards. He runs out to the street and hires a maid or two to help me. It is a gift of God when there is respect.

Hayat H.

He never thwarted my wishes. I did my best never to thwart his. He is still treating me with the same consideration. He never raises his voice with me. He respected me and I treated him like a king. Praise to God. I hope my daughters will have the same luck as I.

Kenza

The perception of a husband's love and respect as a miracle probably stems from the fact that the woman cannot legally demand respect or love. This is illustrated in the list of respective rights and duties in the 1957 Moroccan *Code.*

Art. 36 *The Rights of the Husband Vis-à-Vis His Wife*
1. Fidelity.
2. Obedience according to the accepted standards.
3. Breastfeeding, if possible, of the children born from the marriage.
4. The management of the household and its organization.
5. Deference towards the mother and father and close relatives of the husband.

Art. 35 *The Rights of the Wife Vis-à-Vis Her Husband*
1. Financial support as stated by law, such as food, clothing, medical care, and housing.
2. In case of polygamy, the right to be treated equally with other wives.
3. The authorization to go and visit her parents and the right to receive them according to limits imposed by the accepted standards.

4. Complete liberty to administer and dispose of her possessions with no control on the part of the husband, the latter having no power over his wife's possessions.

Note that the husband owes no moral duties to his wife. Moreover, apart from the rights of the wife listed in numbers 1 and 4 above, all other alleged rights are in fact either restrictions of her freedom (like item 3) or restrictions on her claim on her husband's person (polygamy in item 2). She cannot expect fidelity. What she expects to get from her husband are orders, and what she expects to give is obedience. It is a power relation. This is emphasized and justified by a social order that encourages the husband to command his wife and not to love her, as Ghazali describes.

> Some souls sometimes let themselves be completely over-taken by passionate love [for a woman]. It is pure madness. It is to ignore completely why copulation was created. It is to sink to the level of beasts as far as domination and mastery of oneself go. Because a man passionately in love does not look for the mere desire to copulate, which is already the ugliest of all desires[4] and of which one should be ashamed, but he goes as far as to believe that this appetite cannot be satisfied except with a specific object [a particular woman]. A beast satisfies its sexual appetite where it can, while this type of man [the man in love] cannot satisfy his sexual appetite except with his beloved. Thus he accumulates disgrace after disgrace and slavery after slavery. He mobilizes reason in order for it to serve appetite, while reason was created to command and to be obeyed.[5]

The religious duty of the husband to command his wife is enforced by numerous sayings and proverbs in Moroccan folk-lore, some of which are supposed to be direct quotations from the Prophet and his disciples.

Ask your wife's opinion, but follow your own.

> Ask your wife's opinion, but do the opposite.
> Don't ever follow your wife's suggestions.[6]

The duty of the man to command his wife is embodied in his right to correct her by physical beating. The Koran itself recommends this measure, but only as a last resort. If his wife rebels, the husband is instructed to scold her and then to stop having sexual intercourse with her. Only if these measures fail should he beat her to make her obey.[7] The right of correction, which was thought likely to be used to excess by husbands, was restricted by the Prophet (who was very kind to his wives) to 'decent' proportions.

> Do not beat your wives like one beats a slave and then copulate with them at the end of the night.[8]

Fear of mistreatment and beatings is one of the reasons why girls and their families usually prefer marriage to a husband who lives in the same neighbourhood.

In modern Morocco, women can bring suit against their husbands for beating them. But they have no recourse if they cannot establish physical evidence of mistreatment. Even so, mistreatment must have reached a demonstrably unbearable stage for them to obtain a divorce. It is the judge who must estimate whether the mistreatment is bearable or not and decide whether or not to issue a divorce.[9] Judges are not reputed to favour women in Moroccan society, which means that the right to beat his wife is an almost unchecked privilege of the husband.

In traditional Moroccan society there is no openly admitted behaviour pattern for the wife to express her physical love for her husband, while an openly admitted behaviour pattern for her rejection of him does exist: the *karh*. If, after the first few days of marriage, the wife does not like her husband, she is said to become *harjat karha*, or 'hateful'. This is expressed by ritualized behaviour, usually, according to my interviews, a complete refusal to share space with him (she will leave the room whenever her husband steps in) or to communicate with him verbally. When the wife is *karha*, it is considered a catastrophe by the respective families and by the individuals involved. The woman's rejection of her husband, in spite of the usually binding nature of marriage for women, often ends in the breaking of the marriage bond. The experience of one woman who was married when she was thirteen reveals that the parents who arrange the marriage, contrary to what one might think, are very concerned about their daughter's fate if their plans fail. Women are usually remarried soon after the *karha* experience and often block it out of their memories, as is illustrated in the following interview.

'Zahra and Hamid don't have the same father.'

'What do you mean? Who is Hamid's father then?'

'My first husband.'

'You promised to tell the story of your life, and you forget something as important as that?'

'I really forgot it. It is not important anyway. I don't like to talk about it.'

'How long did it last?'

'He was our neighbour. His wife died and my parents arranged the marriage. When he got in the *dahshousha*[10] I hated him. It lasted one year and a half. I spent most of the time in my parents' house. He did everything he could to make me love him, but when he tried to get near me, it used to aggravate things. When I got pregnant, that was it. I'd see him and I'd start shivering. We organized my running away. My father arranged for me to go and stay with an uncle who was living far away from town. The judge got involved in the affair. My father started sending delegations of *shorfas* [people who think they are, and are believed to be, direct descendants of the Prophet] to my husband's family. Finally, my poor father decided to buy my freedom, and I was liberated!'

Tamou T.

Imam Ghazali agrees that marriage is equivalent to slavery for the woman because it places her in a situation in which she 'has to obey him [her husband] without restrictions, except in cases where what he asks her to do constitutes a flagrant violation of Allah's orders.'[11]

Why does Moroccan society encourage the husband to assume the role of master instead of lover? Does love between man and wife threaten something vital in the Muslim order? We have seen that sexual satisfaction is considered necessary to the moral well-being of the believer. There is no incompatibility between Islam and sexuality as long as sexuality is expressed harmoniously and is not frustrated. What Islam views as negative and anti-social is woman and her power to create *fitna*. Heterosexual involvement, real love between husband and wife, is the danger that must be overcome.

The Prevention of Intimacy

The sexual act is considered polluting[12] and is surrounded by ceremonials and incantations whose goal is to create an emotional distance between the spouses and reduce their embrace to its most elementary function, that of a purely reproductive act. During coitus, the male is actually embracing a woman, symbol of unreason and disorder, anti-divine force of nature and disciple of the devil. Hence a dread of erection, which is experienced as a loss of control and, according to Ghazali,[13] referred to as darkness in verse 3 of sura 113:

> Say: I seek refuge in the lord of daybreak
> From the evil of that which he created
> From the evil of darkness when it is intense.

In an attempt to prevent a complete merging with the woman, the coital embrace is surrounded by a ceremony which grants Allah a substantial presence in the man's mind during intercourse. The coital space is religiously oriented: the couple should have their heads turned away from Mecca. 'They should not face the "holy shrine" in respect for it.'[14] This symbolism of spatial orientation expresses the antagonism between Allah and the woman. Mecca is the direction of God. During intercourse, the man is reminded that he is not in Allah's territory, whence the necessity to invoke his presence.

> It is advisable for the husband to start by invoking God's name and reciting 'Say God is one' first of all and then reciting the *takbir* 'God is most great' and the *tahlil* 'There is no god but God' and then say, 'In the name of God, the high and powerful, make it a good posterity if you decide to make any come from my kidney.'[15]

At the crucial moment of ejaculation, when the physical and spiritual boundaries of the lover threaten to melt in a total identification with the woman,[16] the Muslim lover is reminded

> It is suitable to pronounce without moving the lips, the following words: 'Praise be to God who created man from a drop of water.'[17]

The conjugal unit presents an even graver danger than ephemeral sexual embrace; erotic love has the potential to grow into something much more encompassing, much more total. It can evolve into an emotional bond giving a man the plenitude that 'only God is supposed to give'.

> The erotic relation seems to offer the unsurpassable peak of the fulfilment of the request for love in the direct fusion of the souls of one to the other. . . . A principal ethic of religious brotherhood is radically and antagonistically opposed to all this. From the point of view of such an ethic, this inner earthly sensation of salvation by mature love competes in the sharpest possible way with the devotion of a supramundane God . . .[18]

The Muslim God requires a total love from his subjects; he requires all the believer's capacity for emotional attachment.

> Yet of mankind are some who take unto themselves [objects of worship which they set as] rivals to Allah, loving them with a love like [that which is due] Allah [alone] those who believe are stauncher in their love for Allah.[19]

Or, again:

Emotional attachment divides man's heart, and Allah hath not created man with two hearts within his body.[20]

Muslim monotheism was consolidated in fierce warfare against 'associationism', the predominant religious practice in Arabia during the early seventh century. Idolatry, and therefore the recognition of a multiplicity of incarnations of the divine, the 'association' of various gods and goddesses, was the most widespread belief. Allah was worshipped as one god among others. Islam therefore had to purge the Arab heavens of any other divinity that might threaten Allah's monopoly. Hence the opening statement of the Muslim profession of faith: 'There is no god but God [Allah].' (In this regard, see Ibn Hisham's *Sira*, Ibn al-Khali's *Kitab al-Asnam*, and other works on the native religions of pre-Islamic Arabia.)

The Muslim god is known for His jealousy, and He is especially jealous of anything that might interfere with the believer's devotion to him.[21] The conjugal unit is a real danger and is consequently weakened by two legal devices: polygamy and repudiation. Both institutions are based on psychological premises that reveal an astonishing awareness of the couple's psychology and its weaknesses.

Folk wisdom perceives polygamy as a means by which men make themselves valuable, not by perfecting any quality within themselves, but simply by creating a competitive situation between many females.

Tamou is a treasure chest [Tamou is a woman's name]; Aisha is the key to it [Aisha is another woman's name].[22]

Polygamy in this sense is a direct attempt to prevent emotional growth in the conjugal unit, and results in the impoverishment of the husband's and wife's investment in each other as lovers.

The obvious consequence of polygamy is that the wife does not 'own her husband', she shares him with one or more co-wives. What does this mean? For one thing, it must mean that the polygamous husband tends to have a less emotional investment in any single wife. He does not have 'all his eggs in one basket'. The meaning for the co-wives is less clear. I suspect that polygamy has a general 'lowering effect' on the emotional importance of the husband-wife bond and that this applies to the wife as well as to the husband. She also invests less in her husband and invests more in other relationships.[23]

The meaning of polygamy for the co-wives is clarified by Salama, a sixty-year-old woman who lived as a concubine in a Moroccan harem from 1924 to 1950.

I was happy to be raised to the status of his lover but I was afraid of all the dangers attached to it.[24]
(What dangers?)
Many, the most frightening is the *hjar*.[25]
(Did he ever *hjar* any of you?)
Yes, he did. Zahra. He only solicited her once and never talked to her after that. I was obsessed by Zahra's case. Every time I went to his apartments, I lay there wide awake in the dawn asking myself, 'Is it the last time he is to call me?' I was no different from Zahra. Zahra was more beautiful than many of us. Why will he choose me again?
(Were you jealous?)
You're joking. Jealous of whom? And of what? We had no rights. No one had any rights over him, including the legitimate wife. For once we were all equal. Democracy.

Harems are not exceptional in modern Muslim societies plagued by economic problems. Polygamy is dying statistically,[26] but its assumptions are still at work even within monogamous households, as is illustrated by one of the interviews.

He keeps repeating that he will get a new wife. He threatens me every morning. I do not worry anymore. He is unable to support us. He cannot do anything anymore. How can he put up with one of those modern women? It would be a circus, but it hurts me when he says that, and I feel like hurting him back.

Maria M.

Muslim polygamy, although generally thought of as a male privilege, contains a subtle institutional detail that prevents the male from exercising his most intimate prerogative: the right to have intercourse with whichever wife he desires at any particular moment.

> It is necessary for the polygamous husband to observe equality among his wives and not favour one at the expense of the others. If he leaves for a journey and wants one of them to accompany him, he has to draw lots as the Messenger used to do, and if he frustrates a wife from the night due to her, he should replace it by another night. This is a religious duty. . . . The Prophet (salvation upon him), because of his noble sense of justice and his virile vigour, used to have intercourse with all his other wives when he felt the desire to sleep with a woman who was not the one he was supposed to spend the night with according to the rotation system. That is how, according to Aisha [the youngest of the Prophet's wives and the one he loved the most], he performed such a task in one single night. According to Anas (salvation upon him), the Prophet's nine wives received his conjugal visit in one single morning.[27]

The Prophet's sexual prowess was considered part of his outstanding personality. He was supposed to have the miraculous sexual vigour of forty men,[28] but the ordinary believer is not expected to live up to the Prophet's example. Pragmatism is a Muslim quality and the strict application of the rotation system, for the average man, who could not satisfy nine women in one morning, means that he must refrain from giving in to sexual desire when it involves a woman not indicated by the rotation schedule. This ensures scarcity in the midst of plenty. Not only does it oblige the male to scatter his emotional involvement, but it reinforces the rule of interchangeability. It obliges him to have intercourse with women he does not desire and forbids him from yielding to the attraction of another woman even though she is his own wife.

The underlying assumptions of polygamy also apply to

repudiation. Like polygamy, repudiation seems to be a male privilege allowing the man to change partners by the simple verbal pronunciation of the formula, 'I repudiate thee'. But it is a boomerang. It works against the man as much as for him.

Letter 1

Fez, July 1971
Praise to God.
From Mr._____
To your highness the great religious scholar Moulay Mustapha Alaoui,

I am happy to come before your highness asking your advice concerning a catastrophe which has befallen me, a problem whose solution is beyond my capacity.

I pronounced the repudiation formula while I was boiling with anger. I pray your highness to tell me if there is anything I can do to have my wife back in spite of what has happened.

I must confess that I love my wife deeply and intensely.

Peace.

It is specified in the Moroccan code that a repudiation pronounced in anger or drunkenness is not valid. Although this is quite well known among average Moroccans, this husband seems to feel a need for reassurance in a society in which words have such fatal importance. The husband's anxiety is echoed in the woman's fear of living in a state of illicitness with her own husband whenever he yields to the temptation to use the repudiation formula.

Letter 2

Casablanca,
From Mrs._____
I had a quarrel with my husband and he repudiated me. Now I came back to him but he did not perform the legal formalities for our remarriage. Can I still stay with him or do I have to go to my parents' home? I have three children and he always keeps swearing, using the repudiation formula without ever performing the necessary acts to

make our life lawful again. I have to add I married him very young. Do I have to put up with this situation or can I leave and go back to my parents?

Repudiation is not only a trap for the man and the woman, it also morally binds all members of the family, who feel uncomfortable when they have witnessed a verbal repudiation. If the man does not perform the legal remarriage, they feel that they are living with fornicators who are committing *zina*.

Letter 4

Province of Beni Mellal, 14 May 1971
I am bringing to your attention this problem on behalf of Mr._____

A man said to his wife, 'you are repudiated a triple repudiation' and he repeated it three times. It was a banal misunderstanding. He has children with his wife. She is still living with him in the house. He does not sleep with her or come near her to talk with her. But he still performs all his duties as a father: he gives her the money she needs for herself and for the children.

Now, given the fact that this man is ignorant, that he does not have any knowledge about these religious matters, it is his father who is asking you about what the religious laws say about this problem. Is there a way for this man to have his wife back or is there no solution?

The striking thing about Moroccan divorce is that there is no check whatsoever on the desire of the husband to break the marital bond. The judge's role is limited simply to registering that desire, never contesting it.

The structural instability inherent in the Muslim family has been identified by psychiatrists[29] and pedagogues[30] as having disastrous effects on child development. This instability is likely to increase with the increasing pressures of modernization, which create additional conflicts and tensions. A question like that of the woman's right to go outside the home, which was unequivocally submitted to the husband's authorization in traditional households, is likely to become a source of confusion and conflict between husband and wife. Traditional patterns of heterosexual behaviour, ideology, folk wisdom, and law cannot be of any help to the male whose rights and privileges over his wife are challenged by modernization.

The Mother-in-Law

In a traditional marriage, the mother-in-law is one of the greatest obstacles to conjugal intimacy. The close link between mother and son is probably the key factor in the dynamics of Muslim marriage. Sons too involved with their mothers are particularly anxious about their masculinity and especially wary of femininity.

Psychoanalytic theory has identified the relationship with the mother as a determining factor in the individual's ability to handle a heterosexual relationship.[1] Cross-cultural studies like Philip Slater's have shown that societies have found ways to use this relationship very effectively. Slater divides societies according to the importance they place on the mother-son relationship.

> Societies vary between two poles, one of which accents the mother-child relationship, the other the marital bond. Each produces its own pattern of self-maintaining circularity.[2]

He argues that in societies that institutionalize a weak marital bond, the mother-son relationship is accorded a particularly important place and vice versa. In Muslim societies not only is the marital bond weakened and love for the wife discouraged, but his mother is the only woman a man is allowed to love at all, and this love is encouraged to take the form of life-long gratitude.

> His mother beareth him with reluctance, and bringeth him forth with reluctance, and the bearing of him and the weaning of him is thirty months till, when he attaineth full

strength and reacheth forty years, he saith, My Lord, arouse me that I may give thanks for the favour where-with.[3]

The son's grateful love for the mother is the object of many verses.[4] Moreover, this love is not limited in time. It is not a process with a beginning, a middle and a ritualized end, indicating that the adult male can now engage in a heterosexual relationship with his wife. On the contrary, in a Muslim society, marriage, which in most societies is invested with a kind of initiation ritual allowing the adult son to free himself from his mother, is a ritual by which the mother's claim on the son is strengthened. Marriage institutionalizes the Oedipal split between love and sex in a man's life.[5] He is encouraged to love a woman with whom he cannot engage in sexual intercourse, his mother; he is discouraged from lavishing his affection on the woman with whom he does engage in sexual intercourse, his wife.

The Mother's Decisive Role in the Choice of Her Son's Bride

According to my interviews with traditional women, it is the mother, not the son, who initiates the marriage and makes the decisions about the creation of her son's new family, although officially this is supposed to be the role of the son's father.

> One day we were sitting in the courtyard as usual when somebody knocked at the door. An aunt of mine, my father's cousin, who was to later become my *hma* [mother-in-law] was at the door. She came straight from Tetuan. She was looking for a bride for her son. . . . I was thirteen years old then. She saw me, talked with my father, asked him for my hand for her son and left. She came back two months later and my marriage contract was signed.
> (Did you know your husband?)
> No. I never talked to him.
>
> Fatiha F.

Appearances exaggerate the role of the father-in-law, who is responsible for the negotiations about the bride-price and the execution of financial decisions called for by the marriage contract, but the mother's role is pivotal, because she has access to information relevant to the marriage that only women can have in a sexually segregated society. The mother is the one who can see the bride, engage in discussions with her, and eventually acquire a very intimate knowledge of her body. In Moroccan society only a woman can see another woman naked and gather information about her health. This occurs in a *hammam* (a kind of Turkish bath), which has manifold functions besides allowing people to perform the purification rituals and bathe. The *hammam* is an intense communication centre,[6] a powerful information agency exposing the secrets of the families who frequent it.

The *guellassa* (cashier) and the *teyyaba* (the 'girl friday' who assists the clientele in all sorts of ways, giving massages, carrying water, suggesting herbal recipes for uterine troubles) have a strategic position in the *hammam*. They have more or less complete biographical accounts of the members of the families living around the *hammam*. The young girls are a particular target for gossip, and their behaviour is a daily object of concern to the other women, those who are related to them and those who are not. A young girl's reputation has a direct impact on her family's honour and prestige. It is interesting to note that the women who are in charge of making young girls' reputations—be they mothers-in-law, *guellassas, teyyabas,* or simply relatives of the son—are all elderly women who no longer have any sexual life, because they are widowed or divorced or simply abandoned by husbands involved with younger wives. The power of the elderly woman as receiver and broadcaster of information about young women gives her tremendous power in deciding who will marry whom and significantly reduces the man's decision-making role. If the mother comes up with information about the future bride's bad breath, or a hidden physical deformity, or a skin disease, she is likely to have a decisive influence in the matter. One such example was provided by Maria M., a 55-year-old woman whose marriage was postponed for seven years because the husband's mother told him that she suspected that his future bride had tuberculosis, given her extreme pallor and thin build. Because the fathers of the bride and groom were close friends, such information did not break off the prospect of the marriage altogether, but it did have a mighty influence on the future bride's life.

> I was an old maid by everybody's standards when I got married. All my younger sisters were engaged and got married before me. My marriage became a kind of joke and I felt I was the object of a divine curse. This is why I never open my mouth and say bad things when I am asked my opinion about a young girl. This happened years ago, but I remember the humiliation as vividly as if it happened yesterday. I still cannot smile at my husband's mother.
>
> Maria M.

The power of elderly women over the lives of young people is acknowledged by Moroccan folk wisdom, which views age as having entirely opposite effects on men and women.

> A man who reaches eighty becomes a saint,
> A woman who reaches sixty is on the threshold of hell.[7]

Or:

> What takes Satan a year to do
> Is done by the old hag within the hour.[8]

For a woman, advanced age is synonymous with the power to plot and weave intrigues.

> When the woman grows old
> She becomes obsessed with intrigues;
> Whatever she sees, she wants to get involved in.
> May God curse her, alive or dead.[9]

Before going any further, I should point out that even though the mother seems to be favoured as a woman in Moroccan society, she does not escape the fate of being associated with the devil, the destructive force in the system. Elderly women, as is illustrated by the proverbs, are viewed negatively, exactly like young women, whom society endows with a destructive potential. The only difference is that young women are destructive because they are sexually appealing, old women because they can no longer claim sexual fulfilment. Great pressures are put on the menopausal woman to regard herself as an asexual object and to renounce her sexuality as early as possible. Her husband is expected to turn his attention to younger women — so much so that a menopausal woman who tries to claim her sexual rights with her husband will be perceived as unrealistic and her complaints will be met with scepticism by men and women alike. A current joke that seems to have a lasting appeal for male Moroccan audiences runs:

> Why doesn't the government create a kind of 'used car dealership' for women where you can bring in the old wife, add some money and trade her in for a new one.

It is only by understanding the pressure on the aging woman to renounce her sexual self and conjugal future that one can understand the passion with which she gets involved in her son's life.

> In societies where sex antagonism is strong, the status of women low, and penis-envy therefore intense, the woman's emotional satisfactions will be sought primarily in the mother-son relationship; while in those societies in which these social characteristics are minimally present, the marital bond will be the principal avenue of need-gratification.[10]

In my data, all mothers-in-law were perceived as completely asexual. In a few cases in which information about sleeping arrangements was available, the 'old couple', although sharing the same room, did not share the same bed.

The Mother-in-Law as Friend and Teacher

The mother-in-law and the wife should be considered competitors, but also collaborators. The older woman has many things to offer the young, inexperienced bride, not only in matters concerning sex and pregnancy, but also in other matters vital to a Moroccan woman's life, such as physical beauty. The following quotation illustrates this aspect of the relationship between wife and mother-in-law.

> You see, with all that she did to me, with all her tyranny, I remember my mother-in-law with peace. I do not feel any resentment towards her. With time I came to see her in a more complex way. I realize now how complex a person she was. . . . For example, she was very elegant, always dressed up and seated with a lot of poise and majesty, with her jewelry and her neat headgear. Clean and smart. . . . She always wanted us to be elegant, well-dressed, so that people would not say that she had sloppy brides. . . . She was terribly refined.
>
> Fatiha F.

The secrets of refinement, elegance and adornment are valuable in a society that emphasizes the importance of physical beauty and values aristocratic *savoir-vivre*. An important part of the knowledge society bequeaths to the female child are the vast and diverse techniques and recipes for the use of plants, flowers, seeds, and minerals to make facials, shampoos, and cosmetics. Most Moroccan women still use these traditional beauty techniques in spite of the availability of cheap Western make-up. The mother-in-law's role as imitator of *savoir-vivre* is as important as her role as instructress in matters of birth, sickness, and death.

Moroccan marriage is virilocal. The child-wife leaves her family, either before or immediately after menarche, to live in her husband's household. Because of her segregated upbringing, she is often fearful of men and thus more inclined to trust and to communicate with women. During her first conjugal years she is likely to have a deeper relationship with a mother than with a son:

> 'I stayed with my husband until I had my first period.'
> 'How long did you stay with your husband before you had your first period?'
> 'I don't remember exactly—a year, maybe. I had no breasts, nothing. I was like a boy.'
> 'Did he use to approach you?'
> 'Never. He never approached me until after a whole year.'
> 'And were you living with him and sharing the same room?'
> 'I was living with my *hma* (mother-in-law); I used to cover myself every time I saw him.'
> 'You were living with your *hma*?'
> 'I was living with my *hma*. She used to treat me like a child of hers. She used to go to fetch young girls from the neighbourhood to play with and talk to so that I wouldn't feel bored.'
>
> Kenza

Moroccan parents are reluctant to give their daughters to husbands who live in different localities, for fear of mistreatment. Usually these fears are allayed if the mother of the groom decides to live with her son. To the bride's parents, distrustful of the husband, the presence of the mother-in-law seems to guarantee their daughter's fair treatment.

The following case of a husband-son from the province of Berkane provides an illustration—unusual even by Moroccan standards—of the extent to which a mother may become involved in her daughter-in-law's life.

> Province of Berkane, 20 May 1971
> To Moulay Mustapha Alaoui:
> Dear Sir,
>   I am the father of three children, all of whom were breast-fed *regularly* by my mother, who lost her husband— i.e., my father—a long time ago. She did that because she had milk in her breast.
>   What does religious law stipulate about this breast-feeding?

Not all mothers-in-law are gifted with the lacteal potential of this one, and the take-over of conjugal affairs need not be this extreme. It usually takes the form of the mother-in-law's assisting the young bride during her first several pregnancies.

The interviews reveal that pregnancy is experienced as the submission of the woman's body to strange forces. One could almost speak of dissociative reflexes in women's perceptions of their swollen bodies.

> I became pregnant while still a child myself. I did not want people to see my belly. I wanted to hide it. I would sit so that people would not notice it. I spent whole days crying— just lying about and crying.
>
> Kenza

> I did not know what was happening when the child started moving inside my belly. I would start screaming every time it happened. I had the impression that he was trying to come out of my skin. I felt very strange.
>
> Hayat H.

The perception of first pregnancies as bizarre phenomena is heightened by unpredictable miscarriages.

> 'I did not have my period during the first months that I was married. I was pregnant—a strange pregnancy. By the eighth month my belly was very swollen—a strange feeling, as if it were only fat . . . strange pregnancy. One day I felt the labour, the pain. I had a haemorrhage that lasted for days. I told the people around me that I felt as though a frog was jumping in me, eating my heart. They answered, "It is nothing. You are just too young to know and be patient with pregnancy. What you feel is natural for women." I was not convinced. My husband took me to a doctor. She was a woman. She gave me shots right in the belly. After that I felt very odd and started shivering. Whatever was in my belly was dead. It started coming out. It was not a child. It was a strange accumulation of odd pieces.'

'Odd pieces?'

'Yes, pieces with strange shapes. It was not a child, but odd and different pieces. There were seven in all. One piece was like a fish, another like a grape, a white grape. Another was like an artichoke head; when you pushed on it a white head came out like an egg.'

Fatiha F.

For the first years of marriage, the bride perceives her life as a succession of pregnancies and later recalls these years as ones during which she was entirely devoted to her children and their problems: *Kunt haida felwlad* is a frequent sentence: 'I was preoccupied with children.' The mother-in-law emerges during these years as a beneficent supervisor whose assistance allows the household to function efficiently. Let us analyse the form of this assistance and its effect on the power structure of the domestic unit, focusing on the case of Fatiha F., a 45-year-old wife and mother married to a *petit fonctionnaire* whose job with the Ministry of Justice has required him to live in different parts of Morocco.

The Mother-in-Law's Control Over the Household

The wife's submission to the mother-in-law is required by modern law, which obliges her to 'show deference towards the mother, father and close relatives of the husband'.[11] Since Moroccan households are often deserted by males, the mother-in-law is the only person the wife has to confront daily. This submission is usually expressed in two rituals: the hand-kissing ceremony and the wife's duty to call her mother-in-law *Lalla* (mistress).

> . . . I did not tell the best of it at all, the hand-kissing ceremony. We [the son's wives] had to kiss her hand twice a day, in the morning and after sunset. You kiss her hand on both sides of course. And we had to call her *Lalla*. When I sometimes forgot that hand, the world was turned

upside down. She would engineer a whole show. She wouldn't say anything to me directly to remind me of my duties. Oh no! That was too crude, not subtle enough for her. When my husband came home, she would attack him: 'Do you know something', she would say, 'your wife is getting insolent. I have to put up with her insolence in silence because I love you and I don't want to create problems.' 'Mother', my husband would ask, 'what did she do?' 'Son, today she forgot to kiss my hand at sunset. She is taking more and more liberties with the rules.'

> Fatiha F.

These deference ceremonies express the allocation of power within the domestic unit. The symbol of that power is the key to the storage room where staples and food are kept. The person who has the key is the one who decides what and when to eat.

My *hma* was in charge of everything. She had the power to decide what to eat, the quality and quantity, and she had the key. I could not use food except with her permission. We did the cooking of course. But once the food was ready we were not allowed to touch it. She would come into the kitchen and distribute it according to her own set of priorities. For example, on the eve of festivals we would spend nights making cookies. But we were not allowed to take any for our own use, not even for our own children. Everything was stored by her. I could not even have a cup of tea if I felt like it aside from ritual meal times. I had to beg her for a piece of sugar and some twigs of mint. [Moroccan tea is made of green tea, fresh mint, and sugar.]

> Fatiha F.

Goffman identified several variables in the power structure of totalitarian institutions. One of them is that the managers of the institutions make it impossible for the managed to obtain simple everyday things such as cigarettes or a cup of tea or coffee without submitting to the humiliating process of soliciting permission.[12] In the Moroccan household, besides begging for food, the wife must ask for permission and money to go to the *hammam*. (The *hammam* is a semi-public institution whose normal price does not exceed twenty cents.) On such occasions, bickering and subtle blackmail on the part of the mother-in-law may occur.

> My *hma* was the treasurer, and a very whimsical one too. Sometimes I would go to her and express my intention to visit the *hammam*. However, before asking I would make sure that my husband had already given her the money for it. She would wait until I had prepared everything [it is a lengthy process involving the preparation of facials, home-made shampoos, and so on]. I would put on my *jellaba*, veil my face, and go to her. She would then change her mind and say, 'Do you really have to go? Can't you heat water and bathe here?' I would take off my *jellaba*, take off my veil, and sit down without uttering a word, no protest. I could not protest. To protest you have to have somebody's support; you have to have your parents' support. I did not have that. So I thanked God for the fate He chose for me and shut my mouth.
>
> Fatiha F.

The competition between mother and wife for the son's favours is clearly institutionalized by the son's duty to give his mother whatever he gets for his wife.

> My husband could not give me a gift. Suppose he wanted to give me a scarf. He would say, 'Fatiha, I would like to see you in a red scarf, it will match your complexion.' I would answer that I would be very happy to have one. He would go to the store, but he would have to buy four scarves—one for his mother, two for his divorced sisters, and finally one for me. He couldn't give me the red scarf directly; he had to give them to his mother. She then chose what she wanted for herself and her daughters and gave me the last one. It could be green or black.
>
> Fatiha F.

My husband could not come near me before going to greet
his mother. Once he wanted to surprise me. He bought me
a bra and hid it in his pocket before going to greet his
mother. She noticed that he had something in his pocket
and she laughingly took the bra out of his pocket and
made fun of him: 'I didn't know you started using a bra,
like a woman. She [the wife] has eaten your brain. You act
like a crazy man now [to get things for the wife only].
Where did you drink it? [The reference is to witchcraft
done by the wife to make her husband love her.] Did you
drink it in the soup? Or was it discreetly mixed in your
cookies?'

This sort of incident is a favourite subject for playwrights in
Morocco. One of the most despised personages in the popular
theatre is the mother-in-law.

In a traditional setting the mother's involvement with her son
is not limited to material things. It goes so far as to prevent his
being alone with his wife. A husband and wife cannot be
together during the day without being conspicuously anti-
social.

The social space in a family dwelling is centred on one focal
room, al-bit al-kbir (the big room). It is here that everything
happens and that everyone is encouraged to spend most of their
time. Individual privacy is vehemently discouraged. One of the
accepted gestures for showing dissent within the family is to
refuse to come to this communal room, to shut oneself off in
another room. Leaving the communal room right after dinner is
considered especially rude in traditional households. It is therefore 'natural' for the mother-in-law to use this custom to keep
her son with her for as long as possible.

'Often late in the evening, I felt very sleepy, but I could
not leave the communal room to go to sleep in mine.
Neither could my husband, even if both of us were dying
of fatigue. We still had to sit there with her and wait until
she decided to go to bed. Then we would run to ours. I
could not retire to my room before her. We could not close
our door in her face.'

'And what if it is your husband who takes the initiative to go to bed?'

'Impossible. He can't. You want her to explode? When he used to come very early to the house after work, she would turn to him and say, "Why did you come home so early? Isn't there any fun in the streets? Aren't there women in the streets? Aren't there amusements? Cinemas? Why do you have to come home so early? Men should not be always near their wives. It is a very ugly habit." Often we go to sleep and I can hear her roaming around the windows, trying to listen to our noises, in case I was trying to tell him what happened during the day. I was not crazy enough to tell him secrets, knowing that she was spying on us. One day I forgot to shut the window properly. So when she leaned on it, the door fell ajar under her weight.'

'Did she ever try to join you in bed?'

'Not in our own house, but when we were invited to go somewhere, we spent the night together in the same room.'

Fatiha F.

When the couple decides to leave the extended family, they often seek a government transfer as an escape if the man is a civil servant, thus hiding their desire for privacy under a legitimate cloak. The wife perceives the government's decision to transfer the husband to another locality as an opportunity to recover some power over her life and her husband, and the mother-in-law perceives such a decision as a plot against her.

My husband was busy trying to get us out of there [the extended family, which included the father, the father's brother's family, and two of his sons' families]. He was lobbying to have himself transferred to another part of the country by government decision. It was the only solution compatible with his obedience and respect for his mother.

He lobbied so well that he got his transfer. He was ordered to go to Fedala. But he had to disclose the news to his mother. One day he decided to talk to her. He told her that he was forced by the government to go to Fedala [forty miles away] and that he had no choice but to follow the government decision if he was to keep his job. 'Are you joking?' she said. 'You don't have to leave us. You can commute. Many people commute. It does not seem to kill them. Don't think about leaving. That's out of the question.' He then came to me and said, 'Fatiha, look. Do you want to leave this house at any cost?' 'Yes', I said. 'Listen', he said, 'this is our only chance to escape. I am not going to wait any longer. I am going to speed up the transfer decision. I am going to rent a room, any room. I do not want to hear you complain about how ugly that room might be, or how rough life is going to be for us. And it is going to be financially tough for a long period. Are you ready to put up with that without complaining?' 'Any slum', I whispered, 'will be a palace for us alone.'

He came one day very late and managed to isolate himself with me and whispered, 'Start packing. We are going to leave very soon. I will announce it at the last minute, so as to take her by surprise. Start packing very discreetly.'

I can't tell you what I felt then. I lost my appetite. I lost my tongue. It was both joy and fear. Have you ever experienced joy and fear together? I fasted for two days. I could not eat with that secret inside me. I did not know anymore how to behave, how to walk, what to say. He left the house and left me alone. Instead of packing, I went and opened the carpet, which was rolled in a corner. I took my precious drapes [used only during festival days] and hung them on the door. When he came home that night he looked puzzled. He came to me and whispered, looking at the drapes and the carpet, 'Fatiha, are you crazy? What does this mean? I told you to pack.' 'It means', I answered, 'that I don't know anything about your decision, that I am out of it.' I was scared his mother would discover that we were plotting. I did not let him down, really. But it was the only possible and sensible thing to do, although it seemed then as if I was letting him down. 'I don't know anything', I kept repeating to him. Poor thing, he was left to face his mother alone.

    The following day he came in shouting at me, screaming in a voice so loud you could hear from the mosque. 'Fatiha, you have to pack immediately. These dogs in the government have ordered me to spend the night at Fedala. I do not have the right to refuse anymore. Immediately! Do you hear, Fatiha?'

    'But', shouted his mother from her room, 'where will you spend the night? You have a family. They can't treat you that way. You can't stay in the street.' 'Mother', he said, 'they have foreseen everything. They made it impossible for me to delay the transfer decision any longer. They provided me with a house and a truck to transport the luggage. The truck is coming within the hour.'

The anti-privacy structure of Moroccan society facilitates— indeed, almost requires—the mother-in-law's intervention in her son's physical intimacy with his wife. Recognizing this, we can understand the reasons for the Moroccan prejudice against old women, cursed as 'masters of intrigue'. It is the structure that determines everyone's roles and leaves specific outlets for the individual's cravings and wishes. It is the structure that is cruel not the mother-in-law.

The triangle of mother, son, and wife is the trump card in the Muslim pack of legal, ideological, and physical barriers that subordinate the wife to the husband and condemn the heterosexual relation to mistrust, violence and deceit. Young people demanding love-marriages not only create tremendous conflicts with their parents, but also almost always guarantee conflict in their own marriages.

A young man raised in a misogynist society will tend, unless he is lucky enough to undergo a radical cultural revolution, to manifest fear of women in his relation with the wife he has chosen and may even desire to love. And although many material things have changed dramatically in Muslim societies, there has been no cultural upheaval at all. All attempts to bring about serious breaches in traditional ideology or to abandon traditional cultural models concerning the family are denounced as atheist deviations (given the religious character of the *Muduwana*, an extension and incarnation of the *shari'a*), as *bida'* ('innovations', the connotation being negative), and as betrayals of *asala* (authenticity).

A chasm has therefore been widening between the necessities imposed by modern family life and the patterns that are supposed to shape relations within that institution. Although the economic and spatial foundations of the traditional family (based on sexual segregation) have suffered severe shocks with the integration of the Moroccan economy into the international market, we may none the less expect neurotic attempts to freeze traditional superstructures, to preserve the traditional patterns and concepts that govern family relations. The result is conflict, tension, and break-ups among young couples, exactly because they are trying to build something different from the stifling sexual relations idealized by tradition.

The higher the aspirations, the greater the psychological cost. By examining the changes that have occurred (in particular in the spatial dimension), we can identify some of the current conflicts between men and women that result from this gap between the shifting infrastructure and the rigid ideological superstructure.

The Meaning of Spatial Boundaries

Muslim sexuality is territorial: its regulatory mechanisms con-
sist primarily in a strict allocation of space to each sex and an
elaborate ritual for resolving the contradictions arising from the
inevitable intersections of spaces.[1] Apart from the ritualized
trespasses of women into public spaces (which are, by definition,
male spaces), there are no accepted patterns for interactions
between unrelated men and women. Such interactions violate
the spatial rules that are the pillars of the Muslim sexual order.
Only that which is licit is formally regulated. Since the interaction of unrelated men and women is illicit, there are no rules
governing it. Those people now experiencing sexual desegregation are therefore compelled to improvise. And whereas
imitation is possible, creation is far more difficult.

Boundaries are never established gratuitously. Society does
not form divisions purely for the pleasure of breaking the social
universe into compartments. The institutionalized boundaries
dividing the parts of society express the recognition of power in
one part at the expense of the other.[2] Any transgression of the
boundaries is a danger to the social order because it is an attack
on the acknowledged allocation of power. The link between
boundaries and power is particularly salient in a society's
sexual patterns.

> Patterns of sexual dangers can be seen to express sym-
> metry or hierarchy. It is impossible to interpret them as
> expressing something about the actual relation of the
> sexes. I suggest that many ideas about sexual dangers are
> better interpreted as symbols of the relation between parts
> of society, as mirroring designs of hierarchy or symmetry
> which apply in the larger social system.[3]

The symbolism of sexual patterns certainly seems to reflect society's hierarchy and power allocation in the Muslim order. Strict space boundaries divide Muslim society into two sub-universes: the universe of men (the *umma*, the world religion and power) and the universe of women, the domestic world of sexuality and the family. The spatial division according to sex reflects the division between those who hold authority and those who do not, those who hold spiritual powers and those who do not.[4] The division is based on the physical separation of the *umma* (the public sphere) from the domestic universe. These two universes[5] of social interaction are regulated by antithetical concepts of human relations, one based on community, the other on conflict.

Membership of the Two Universes

The Public Universe of the Umma	*The Domestic Universe of Sexuality*
The believers. Women's position in the *umma* universe is ambiguous; Allah does not talk to them directly. We can therefore assume that the *umma* is primarily male believers.	Individuals of both sexes as primarily sexual beings. But because men are not supposed to spend their time in the domestic unit, we may assume that the members are in fact women only.

Principles Regulating Relations Between Members

The Umma	*The Family*
Equality	Inequality
Reciprocity	Lack of Reciprocity
Aggregation	Segregation
Unity, Communion	Separation, Division
Brotherhood, Love	Subordination, Authority
Trust	Mistrust

Communal Relationship

> A social relationship will be so-called 'communal' if and so far as the orientation of social action is based on subjective feeling of the parties, whether affectual or traditional, that they belong together.[6]

The universe of the *umma* is communal; its citizens are persons who unite in a democratic collectivity based on a sophisticated concept of belief in a set of ideas, which is geared to produce integration and cohesion of all members who participate in the unifying task.

Conflict Relationship

> A social relationship will be referred to as a 'conflict' in so far as action within it is oriented intentionally to carrying out the actor's own will against the resistance of the other party or parties.[7]

The citizens of the domestic universe are primarily sexual beings; they are defined by their genitals and not by their faith. They are not united, but are divided into two categories: men, who have power, and women, who obey. Women—who are citizens of this domestic universe and whose existence outside that sphere is considered an anomaly, a transgression—are subordinate to men, who (unlike their women) also possess a second nationality, one that grants them membership of the public sphere, the domain of religion and politics, the domain of power, of the management of the affairs of the *umma*. Having been identified as primarily citizens of the domestic universe, women are then deprived of power even within the world in which they are confined, since it is the man who wields authority within the family. The duty of Muslim women is to obey (as is very clear in the *Muduwana* and in Malik's *al-Muwatta*, from which it is inspired and on which it is based). The separation of the two groups, the hierarchy that subordinates the one to the other, is expressed in institutions that discourage, and even prohibit, any communication between the sexes. Men and women are supposed to collaborate in only one of the tasks required for the survival of society: procreation.

In fact, whenever cooperation between men and women is inevitable, as between the members of a couple, an entire array of mechanisms is set in motion to prevent too great an intimacy from arising between the partners. Sexual segregation thus fuels, and is fuelled by, the conflicts that it is supposed to avoid between men and women. Or better, sexual segregation intensifies what it is supposed to eliminate: the sexualization of human relations.

The Seclusion of Women

In order to prevent sexual interaction between members of the *umma* and members of the domestic universe, seclusion and veiling (a symbolic form of seclusion) were developed. But paradoxically, sexual segregation heightens the sexual dimension of any interaction between men and women.

In a country like Morocco, in which heterosexual encounter is the focus of so many restrictions, and consequently of so much attention, seduction becomes a structural component of human relations in general, whether between individuals of the same sex or between men and women.

I have concentrated my discussion here on heterosexual relations, but our understanding of sexual identity cannot be complete without studies clarifying the interaction among individuals of the same sex. A society that opts for sexual segregation, and therefore for impoverishment of heterosexual relations, is a society that fosters 'homosocial' relations[8] on the one hand and seduction as a means of communication on the other. Seduction is a conflict strategy, a way of seeming to give of yourself and of procuring great pleasure without actually giving anything. It is the art of abstaining from everything while playing on the promise of giving. It is a childish art in that the child has a vital need to protect itself, but for an adult it is the expression of an often uncontrollable emotional avarice. It is very rare that an individual who has invested years in learning seduction as a mode of interchange can suddenly open up and lavish all his (or her) 'emotional treasures' on the person he has finally chosen to love.

In a society in which heterosexual relations are combated, emotional fulfilment is inhibited. As we are taught to fear and mistrust the other sex, and therefore to relate to its members through seduction, manipulation, and domination, we become mere puppets who extend the games of seduction, acceptable during adolescence, into our relations as mature men and women.

The hedonistic enhancement of the beauty of the human body seems to have been a pronounced Mediterranean characteristic of Morocco which Islam failed to curb. Body adornment with both jewelry and cosmetics is an integral part of socialization. Even men, at least the generation now in their sixties, used to wear cosmetics to darken their eyelids (*khol*) and lips (*swak*) for religious rituals and festivals. Islam took an unequivocally negative attitude towards body ornamentation, especially for women.[9] It required pious women to be modest in their appearance and hide all ornamentation and eye-catching beauty behind veils.

> And tell the believing women to lower their gaze and be modest, and to display of their adornment only that which is apparent and to draw their veils over their bosoms, and not to reveal their adornment save to their own husbands or fathers or husband's fathers, or their sons or their husband's sons, or their women, or their slaves, or male attendants who lack vigour or children who know naught of women's nakedness. And let them not stamp their feet so as to reveal what they hide of their adornment. And turn unto Allah together, O believers, in order that ye may succeed.[10]

According to Ghazali, the eye is undoubtedly an erogenous zone in the Muslim structure of reality, just as able to give pleasure as the penis. A man can do as much damage to a woman's honour with his eyes as if he were to seize hold of her with his hands.

> To look at somebody else's wife is a sinful act. . . . The look is fornication of the eye, but if the sexual apparatus is not

set in motion by it [if the man does not attempt to have sexual intercourse], it is a much more easily pardoned act.[11]

When the Prophet was asking God to protect him from the most virulent social dangers, he asked for help in controlling his penis and his eye from the dangers of fornication.[12]

The theory that seclusion in Islam is a device to protect the passive male who cannot control himself sexually in the presence of the lust-inducing female is further substantiated by verse 60 of sura 24, which explains that elderly women (supposed to be unattractive) can go unveiled. Belghiti's survey of rural women, among whom seclusion is the prevailing mode, reveals that the restrictions on women's movements do not apply to elderly women, who consequently have a greater freedom.[13]

The seclusion of women, which to Western eyes is a source of oppression, is seen by many Muslim women as a source of pride.[14] The traditional women interviewed all perceived seclusion as prestigious. In rural Morocco seclusion is considered the privilege of women married to rich men.[15]

Harems, the ultimate form of seclusion, were considered even more prestigious, since they required huge economic assets. One of the women I interviewed, Salama, lived most of her life as a concubine in a harem. This is unusual even by Moroccan standards, and her experience contrasts sharply with that of most women. Because women are not allowed to leave a harem, sexual segregation is more successfully realized there than in the average, monogamous family. Successful seclusion of human beings requires considerable economic investment, because services must be provided at home for the secluded. Other women, who must go out to shop or go to the baths, are under many restrictions outside the home.

The Deseclusion of Women: on the Street

Traditionally, women using public spaces, trespassing on the *umma* universe, are restricted to few occasions and bound by specific rituals,[16] such as the wearing of the veil. The veil is worn by Moroccan women only when they leave the house and walk through the street, which is a male space. The veil means that the woman is present in the men's world, but invisible; she has no right to be in the street.

If chaperoned, women are allowed to trespass into the men's universe on the traditional visits to the *hammam*, the public bath, and to the tomb of the local saint. According to my data, visits to the *hammam* used to be bi-monthly and to the saint's tomb not more than once or twice a year (usually the 27th day of Ramadan). Both required the husband's permission. The chaperoning was entrusted to an elderly asexual woman, usually the mother-in-law.

Traditionally, only necessity could justify a woman's presence outside the home, and no respect was ever attached to poverty and necessity. Respectable women were not seen on the street. In class-conscious Morocco, the maid, who has to go wherever she can to find a job, occupies the lowest rung of the social scale, and to be called a maid is one of the commonest insults. Only prostitutes and insane women wandered freely in the streets. One expression for a prostitute is *rajlha zahqa*, 'a woman whose foot is slipping'. The Pascon-Bentahar survey revealed that when a rural youth visits a town he assumes that any woman walking down the street is sexually available.[17]

Women in male spaces are considered both provocative and offensive. Since schooling and jobs both require women to be able to move freely through the streets, modernization necessarily exposes many women to public harassment.[18]

In *The Hidden Dimension*, Edward Hall made two perceptive remarks about the use of space in Middle Eastern, Arab-Muslim societies. First, 'there is no such thing as an intrusion in public. Public means public.'[19] It is not possible for an individual to claim a private zone in a public space. This seems quite true for Morocco and has a particular bearing on women's presence in the street, as one might guess.

Second, space has a primarily social rather than physical quality. The notion of trespassing is related not so much to physical boundaries as to the identity of the person performing the act.[20] A friend, for example, never trespasses, while a foe always does.

A woman is always trespassing in a male space because she is, by definition, a foe. A woman has no right to use male spaces. If she enters them, she is upsetting the male's order and his peace of mind. She is actually committing an act of aggression against him merely by being present where she should not be. A woman in a traditionally male space upsets Allah's order by inciting men to commit *zina*. The man has everything to lose in this encounter: peace of mind, self-determination, allegiance to Allah, and social prestige.

If the woman is unveiled the situation is aggravated. The Moroccan term for a woman who is not veiled is *aryana* ('nude'), and most women who frequent schools or hold jobs outside the home today are unveiled. The two elements together—trespassing and trespassing in the 'nude'—constitute an open act of exhibitionism.

> Whether the indictable act consists of words spoken, gestures conveyed, or act performed, the communication structure of the event often consists of an individual initiating an engagement with a stranger of the opposite sex by means of the kind of message that would be proper only if they were on close and intimate terms. Apart from psychodynamic issues, exhibitionists often spectacularly subvert social control that keeps individuals interpersonally distant even though they are physically close to each other. The assault here is not so much directly on an individual as on the system of rights and symbols the individual employs in expressing relatedness and unrelatedness to those about him.[21]

The male's response to the woman's presence is, according to the prevailing ideology, a logical response to exhibitionist aggression. It consists in pursuing the woman for hours, pinching her if the occasion is propitious, and possibly assaulting her verbally, all in the hope of convincing her to carry her exhibitionist propositioning to its implicit end.

During the Algerian revolution, the nationalist movement used women to carry arms and messages. One of the problems the revolutionary movement faced was the harassment of these

women by Algerian 'brothers' who mistook them for prostitutes and interfered with the performance of their nationalist
task.[22] A similar incident was reported to have taken place near
a refugee camp in Lebanon.

A female Palestinian militant was performing her task as a
sentinel. She was posted in a deserted spot a few yards away
from the camp, her machine-gun on her shoulder, when a
Lebanese civilian who noticed her came by to make a proposition. When the woman rejected his advances with indignant
words and gestures, the man got angry and said, 'How do you
want me to believe that a woman standing alone in the street
the whole night has any honour?' The woman is said to have
turned her gun towards her suitor and told him, 'I am here in
the street soiling my honour to defend yours because you are
unable to do it yourself.'[23] In spite of its revolutionary setting,
the anecdote reveals that the female militant shares with the
male civilian the belief that her being alone in the street is
dishonourable. Her reflex was to justify her presence in the
male space, not to claim her right to be there.

The Deseclusion of Women: in the Office

The absence of modes of relatedness other than genital encounter helps to explain the form of heterosexual encounters in
offices as well as on the street.

The 'office' is a recent development in Moroccan history, a
legacy of the centralized bureaucracy set up by the French after
1912. After independence, public administration expanded both
in terms of offices and posts and in terms of the portion of
public resources it swallows. The state is now by far the most
important employer in the country. A substantial number of
literate working women are in government offices. These women,
who often have not finished high school, are typists and secre-
taries and usually occupy positions subordinate to their male
colleagues.[24]

The situation of the working woman in the office is reminiscent of her position in a traditional household and on the street.
These conflicting images are likely to stimulate conflicting

patterns of behaviour in men. The boss's typist, like his wife and sister, is in a subordinate position, and he has the right to command her. Like them, she is dependent on him (more or less directly) for economic survival. He administers her salary, which is given to her because she provides him with specific services. Her advancement and promotion depend on him. It is therefore not surprising if he comes to confuse her with the woman he dominates because of his economic superiority and institutional authority (in other words, his wife), a step many men seem to take with ease. In any event, the drift that occurs in relations between the bureaucrat and his secretary, generated by his confusion of his privileges as a man and his rights and privileges as a bureaucrat, are not limited to sexual behaviour. Max Weber identified this confusion as one of the problems of the bureaucratic system.

The confusion is inherent in any bureaucratic structure, but it assumes a particularly exaggerated character in Third World societies in which bureaucratization is relatively recent. Morocco, of course, already had its Makhzencentral, but that institution lacked the structures, resources, equipment, and personnel that it now commands. The harassment of the woman state employee occurs because she has transgressed the boundaries of the male space *par excellence*, the administration of affairs of state. The conflict and tension experienced by women who work in the state administration is proportional to the insolence of their intrusion into the sanctuaries of male power.

Women's increasing encroachment into traditionally male spaces greatly intensifies the sexual aspect of any encounter between men and women, especially in the urban centres. The process of integration of women into the modern circuits of the production system is now quite advanced, however unplanned or even undesired the process may have been. A growing number of women, both educated and illiterate, are invading the labour market and the modern workshops. The aspiration for a *hadma mezyana* (well-paid job) is now shared by poor illiterate women and their more privileged sisters who have gained access to wealth and education.

When women go to work they are not only trespassing in the universe of the *umma* but are also competing with their former masters, men, for the scarce available jobs. The anxiety created by women seeking jobs in the modern sector, and thus demanding a role traditionally reserved for men, inevitably aggravates tension and conflict because of the scarcity of jobs and the high rate of unemployment among men.

9
The Economic Basis of Sexual Anomie in Morocco

One can easily imagine the problems likely to result from the determination of women to invade the labour market in a Muslim society suffering from high unemployment.[1] A society having difficulty creating jobs for men tends to fall back on traditional customs that deny women's economic dimension and define them purely as sexual objects—and to write those customs into law. This is just what happened in Morocco. In 1956–57, at the dawn of independence, a commission of ten men selected from the leading religious authorities and the most prominent functionaries of the Ministry of Justice met and drafted a *Personal Status Code* which, after some discussion, was adopted and became law.[2] Article 115 of that code affirms

> Every human being is responsible for providing for his needs (*nafaqa*) through his own means, with the exception of wives, whose husbands provide for their needs.

The woman's clear and unequivocal right to work is thus nowhere affirmed in this law, which opts instead for the fantasy encouraged by the traditional image of the Muslim woman, an image that confounds virility with economic power and femininity with the passive status of consumer. The law helps to keep alive this fantasy, which draws its great strength from its own lack of reality. In Morocco, racked by class divisions and constant inflation, the man in the street spends considerable time discussing virtually insoluble economic problems. The image of patriarchal virility compels him to consider himself responsible for providing for his own needs as well as for those of his wife and children, and therefore for finding a salary large enough to do this. But the majority of men never manage to find stable and regular jobs, and the majority of women are forced to look for wage-labour outside the family if they are to survive. Nevertheless—and this is the main point I want to look at here—at a time when capitalist appropriation of the country's best land for production of cash-crops for export to the Common Market is well-advanced, at a time when millions of peasant families can no longer make ends meet and are flocking to the urban centres or leaving to work in Europe, at a time of economic cataclysm, we are still brought up on images straight out of Baghdad during the days of the *Arabian Nights*, images of men who lavish pearls and emeralds on the women who surround them.

The individual cannot help but suffer from such a discordance between the realities of everyday life and the ideas and images stamped into people's minds. The wider the gap between reality and fantasy (or aspiration), the greater the suffering and the more serious the conflict and tension within us. The psychological cost is just barely tolerable. The fact that we cling to images of virility (economic power) and femininity (consumption of the husband's fortune) that have nothing whatever to do with real life contributes to making male-female dynamics one of the most painful sources of tension and conflict, for several reasons. The most obvious one is that in the traditional system our identities are primarily sexual. The system of honour binds the reputation of men and women to their genital apparatus. A respectable man is not simply someone who acquires some degree of economic power, but who also controls the sexual behaviour of his wife, daughters, and sisters. But this is possible only if he is able to control their movements, to limit their mobility and thereby to reduce their interaction with the strange men with whom they threaten to 'sully the family's honour'. Once again, money and sex are intimately linked in the definition of identity, for both men and women. New ideological systems have emerged (laws, cultural patterns shaped by literature, education, radio and television), and new identity models too, to guide people through these decades of violent economic and spatial upheavals (including the bankruptcy of the territoriality of sex).

The Moroccan people would be a lot happier, and better off economically as well, if a man's honour and prestige were no longer related to his ability to control his women by stuffing them with chickens and pearls but instead depended on his ability to master solar energy or electronics. Just as they would be happier and better off if a woman's honour and prestige were no longer related to her spatial immobility, her passive role as consumer, but instead depended on her ability to master solar energy or electronics.

One of the basic changes now occurring is the disappearance of the roles attributed to each sex as elaborated and used by tradition for centuries. Sexual desegregation of space is already on the way, and brings with it sexual desegregation of the economy and the dissolution of boundaries between public and private space so vital for social identity. The greatest battles, the most serious misunderstandings, that women have with the men they love concern this fissure between public and private. 'You can do that in public but not in private', 'you shouldn't travel or go out alone at that hour', 'you shouldn't talk to another man, even a colleague of ours, when you're out with your partner', and so on.

But let us return to the original point: the lack of correspondence between real life and the ideas and patterns that are supposed to express it. This lack of correspondence, to use the 'noble' term, is called anomie. According to Durkheim, anomie is a confusion more than an absence of norms. Anomie occurs when

> The moral system which has prevailed for centuries is shaken, and fails to respond to new conditions of human life, without any new system having yet been formed to replace that which has disappeared.[3]

In the case of Moroccan male-female dynamics, sexual desegregation through schooling and the employment of women in non-domestic jobs is a direct attack on the spatial barrier erected by Islam between males and females. But Islam's division of space between the sexes is not an isolated phenomenon; it is the reflection of a specific distribution of power and authority and a specific division of labour, which together form a coherent social order. Moroccan society has not pushed its social reform in matters of male-female relations as far as the changes in the traditional distribution of power and authority might have warranted; hence the anomic aspect of that relation.

The role of the state as a producer of ideology appears more clearly if we contrast Morocco to another traditional society, China, which underwent an entirely different process of change affecting both reality and ideology. During the phase of nationalist struggle (struggle against external hegemony), Mao Zedong analysed the Chinese situation thus

> A man in China is usually subjected to the domination of three systems of authority: 1) the State system (political authority); 2) the clan system (clan authority); and 3) the supernatural system (religious authority). . . . As for women, in addition to being dominated by these three systems of authority, they are also dominated by the men (the authority of the husband). These four authorities . . . are the four thick ropes binding the Chinese people.[4]

One of the first acts of independent China was the promulgation, on 1 May 1950, of the Marriage Law of the People's Republic of China, whose first article states

> The arbitrary and compulsory feudal marriage system which is based on the superiority of men over women and which ignores the children's interests is abolished.

The Chinese man is not burdened by the duty to support his wife as well as himself. The Chinese woman is not limited to biological reproduction and sexual services. She is urged to earn her own living as a productive economic agent. Consequently, the Chinese male is encouraged not to think of himself only as a sexual being, but primarily as an economic agent and a person with multiple potentials and capacities.

Change is a painful process, but it becomes bearable to the individual if the degree of ambiguity and contradiction is lessened by the availability of coherent new behaviour models.[5]

The Chinese husband suffers less than his Moroccan counterpart because the former at least knows exactly what new attitude he is expected to have towards his wife's work.

> Both husband and wife shall have the right to free choice of occupation and free participation in work or in social activities.[6]

The Moroccan husband, on the other hand, is faced with anxiety-provoking ambiguities. This is epitomized in the Moroccan *Code*'s endorsement of the man's right to control his wife's access to the outside world.[7] It is a masterpiece of ambiguity and a mine of potential conjugal discord. In traditional Morocco, the man's prestige is embodied in the seclusion of his female relatives. A man whose wife wanders around the streets free is a man whose masculinity is in jeopardy. Article 35 of the *Code* states that among the woman's rights *vis-à-vis* her husband is the right to visit her parents, implying that she has no other right to leave the house without her husband's permission. Although sexual equality was proclaimed in the Moroccan constitution in the name of equality between all citizens, the right to leave the house, and thus by implication the right to work outside the home (which assumes a particular importance in a traditionally segregated setting), was not granted by Moroccan legislators to the female citizen. On the contrary, the need for women to negotiate such rights with their husbands is emphasized.

Since the system holds—and the law confirms—that a woman's place is in the home and that her access to offices and factories is subject to her husband's authorization, women are reminded whenever they get jobs that it is a privilege and not a right. Moreover, the husband is encouraged to perceive his wife and her salary as belonging to him, since she requires his permission to earn her salary. (In fact, in spite of the 1957 *Code*'s uncompromising stand on the separation of properties and on the woman's uncontested right to manage her own property, the husband's claim to his wife's salary is a recurrent subject of dispute in Moroccan courts.[8])

One can imagine the frustration and resentment the Moroccan

male is likely to experience, trapped as he is between a law that gives him the right to control his wife's movements and the economic necessity that forces her to take a job. The gap between the sexual ideology reflected by the laws and the way most people live their lives is a sign of the absence of a genuine modern moral system.

The nationalist movement, which initiated and supported changes in women's position in society, has failed to carry out its post-independence task of socio-economic regeneration. Whatever the reasons, the unhappy fate of the nationalist movement had disastrous implications for sexual desegregation and the prospects of an integrated women's liberation in which ideology and reality reflect each other in a coherent structure. The present situation is characterized by a flagrant discrepancy between women's newly acquired rights to traditionally male spaces such as streets, offices, and classrooms, and the traditional ideology according to which such rights are clear cases of trespass.

Education for Women

Education for women has been a major factor in sexual desegregation. It is associated with Westernization, but it would be a mistake to attribute it to French influence alone.[9] This idea of France as a 'modernizing' force is a colonial fantasy, since the French protectorate actually helped bring about an astonishing consolidation of traditions and breathed new life into existing hierarchies and inequalities. Here, for instance, is a quotation from a book by André Révérand on General Lyautey, dealing with the general's attitude to Moroccan culture. What fascinated the general, and Révérand after him, was the 'aristocratic' dimension of Moroccan society.

> His [Lyautey's] letter of 29 March 1913 to Wladimir d'Ormesson is a marvellous illustration of the profound meeting of the minds between the Moroccans and the general: the same taste for tradition, the same aristocratic sense, the same respect for hierarchy, the same innate

chivalrous, even 'aristocratic' concept of life. Greeted as a
lord, he received as a lord.[10]

The protectorate, presented even today as a cataclysmic time
of cultural upheaval, actually served as a bridge permitting the
consolidation of hierarchies and the continuation of inegalitarian
ideologies in which sex inequalities played a basic part. (A
feminist reading of the history of the protectorate and independence would clearly reveal the real direction of trends and
ideology during these decades, which are often associated not
with continuity but with change.) French policy, inspired by
General Lyautey, who liked to think of himself as a great
humanist and philosopher, was to respect Moroccan traditions
whenever they were not in open contradiction with French
interests. For example, the traditional landowning system con-
flicted with French interests and was entirely dismantled. But
the Moroccan family structure, which did not conflict, became
the object of an exotic respect. In fact, many of the laws concerning women introduced during the French protectorate com-
pounded the burdens of local traditions with the misogynist
dementia of the Napoleonic Code. The legal articles on obligations and contracts concerning women in financial transactions,
as well as the articles in the penal code on 'crimes of passion',
are gifts of super-patriarchal French civilization and are in
complete contradiction with the principles of the *shari'a.*

The introduction of schooling for girls, for example, cannot be
explained without taking account of the nationalist movement
that swept Morocco's urban centres in the thirties and forties.
At first this movement, as a dissident struggle, was compelled
to challenge all inequalities, including sexual ones. Nationalists
held a particularly optimistic belief in Morocco's ability to
rejuvenate its structures, revitalize itself, shake off futile
anachronisms, and bridge the centuries separating it from the
industrial world. By 1942 schooling for women, unthinkable a
few decades before, was advocated by the nationalists as a
necessity. They wanted to defeat the French at any cost, even if
it meant interfering in the family structure.

Under these circumstances Moroccan girls were pushed into
classrooms, entrusted to male teachers, and allowed to walk

through the streets four times a day. All these events were indeed unusual, but everything was unusual in Morocco in 1942.

> Finally, on the second of the month of Muharram in the year 1362 [that is, November 1942 of the Christian calendar] a Moroccan delegation was received by His Majesty and was given a most warm welcome. He himself saw no problem in allowing men to teach Arabic to Muslim girls. Some days later there was a gathering of young people from Fez, Rabat, and Sale at the Palace where His Majesty was presiding at the Council of Ministers. These young people were admitted to participate in the discussions of the issue at hand. The meeting lasted two hours and the following decisions were made: age for entering school [for girls] 7 years of age; for leaving school 13 years. For the programme of primary education for girls, teachers of Arabic were chosen and designated directly by His Majesty.[11]

The 'young people' who went to see the king about the matter of girls' education were nationalist militants, and 'His Majesty' was Muhammad V, who puzzled the entire country in 1943 when he presented his daughter, Princess Aisha, unveiled before the nation. The liberation of women was considered by the nationalists as an absolutely necessary step in the strategy to defeat the French Christians.

The nationalist leader Allal al-Fasi did not forget women when he participated in drafting an 'Arab Charter' during the same period.

> The state must provide gratuitously a basic minimum in the following spheres:
> a. maternity, motherhood, child care . . .
> The state must ensure to individuals the following rights in the field of production:
> c. . . . enabling women to perform their duties in society.[12]

The number of girls in primary schools rose from 15,080 in 1947,[13] to 186,330 in 1957, and to 423,005 in 1971.[14] The movement for women's education apparently snowballed, because starting in 1945 girls did not leave school at thirteen as had been decided by the nationalists; they had gained access to secondary schools. Seven percent of Moroccan girls between ages 14 and 19 are now in secondary establishments; correspondingly for boys, 14 percent.[15] According to government figures, 92,006 girls were enrolled in secondary schools in 1971, but only a token number of girls made it to the universities.[16] At present the number of women holding primary-school diplomas in the urban centres is higher than the number of men. According to the 'Results of the Inquiry Into Urban Employment' (issued by the Bureau of Statistics in Rabat in 1976), among people more than ten years old 69 percent of females and 63 percent of males have primary-school diplomas. As for secondary schools, despite pressures on young girls to marry early, nearly one-third of them manage to get high-school diplomas (29 percent, compared with 33 percent of boys). Finally, about half of the 4 percent of the urban population that have degrees in higher education are women.

The insistence of Moroccan women in demanding access to education is shown by a number of indicators, in particular their better grades than boys and their unshakeable will to continue their studies after marriage and children. Only a dozen years ago, marriage was regarded as marking an end to any young wife's educational aspirations. But it is now typical, especially among the younger generations, for young women to go back to school after getting married and having children. Happiness in modern Morocco, it seems, requires more than a pretty and nicely made-up face. A solid education has become a necessity, as vital to status as beauty. Female access to education and the job market, especially among the middle class, is one of the most important aspects of the social dynamic in contemporary Morocco.[17]

Even though the rate of schooling of girls seems now to have stabilized after a period of rapid rise, and even though it remains blocked in the rural regions and among the poorer layers, it is nevertheless the case that the infiltration of women into classroom and office, and consequently into the street, represents a wide and radical breach in the traditional system.

Although the percentage of females in school is ridiculously low by Western standards, it would be a mistake to dismiss it as insignificant. Since sexual segregation is primarily a symbolic spatial confinement of women, just a few women strolling along the streets in an unhurried fashion can upset society's psychic equilibrium.

Jobs for Women

Jobs for women, their access to positions in which their contribution is remunerated with a wage, is probably the most striking manifestation of the end of an epoch and a system, even if Moroccan legislators and ideologues continue to lull the population with the myth of the man with the fat wallet who showers his women with exotic fruit and rare jewels. What is new, and laden with consequences, is not the mere fact of women working (Moroccan women of the poor classes have always worked[18]), but the fact that they are working in positions in which they are paid wages. In traditional Moroccan society only women of the plutocracy were inactive and led lives of leisure. The others worked hard, often without any remuneration whatever, in domestic services and also in economic sectors like crafts and agriculture, which were by no means unimportant in the precapitalist economy. The women of Rabat-Salé run an export-oriented crafts industry. If the female peasants of the Rif, of the Doukkala plain, or of the Gharb region decided to stop working both inside and outside the home, the life of these regions would be seriously disrupted. But the colossal daily labour of these women is usually unpaid. One of the most common statuses among the primary sector, or at least among its women, is 'family aid', which means unpaid worker.[19]

What is of interest to us here, then, is not the mere fact that women are working, for only the most simple-minded can continue to claim that Moroccan women 'went out' to work in 1956, the year of independence. Sensible people must place female labour in its historical context. The phrase *lmra lhaddama* (the working woman) refers to women who work in an economic space separate from their domicile and who receive a wage. This is a specific phenomenon—female labour performed outside the home, for an employer wholly foreign to the family, and paid for with a wage—that is not only a novelty but also challenges the sexual division of labour in society. Nevertheless, to grasp the trends of conflict now being generated by the aspirations of Moroccan working women we must first consider the general conditions of female employment as they emerged in the 1971 census.[20]

According to the official census, while the employment rate for men is nearly stagnant, the women's rate has shown a tremendous increase. In the period between 1960 and 1971, this rate increased 75 percent. In urban areas, where women's labour is more easily assessed, the number of working women has doubled.

> Women, encouraged on the one hand by socio-economic changes which are taking place and on the other hand by a rising level of education, are becoming serious competitors to men in the labour market. Out of every 100 active individuals, 30 are young women.[21]

The most striking characteristic of Moroccan female labour is its youth; 44% of working women are under twenty-five, and 15% are under fifteen years old. The corresponding figures for men are 29% and 6%.

In the services sector there are predominantly two kinds of working women, the civil servant and the maid. There are 27,700 women working mainly for the Moroccan government, 15,200 of whom hold teaching jobs. The integration of women into prestigious activities such as teaching, health, and finance is of particular importance precisely because the bulk of working women are illiterate or semi-literate.

Lack of education forces most women into subordinate positions, under men's supervision, hardly different from their traditional situations. Maids, for example, occupy such a traditional subordinate position. They are remarkable not only for their numbers (100,200), but also for their age distribution— more than half the maids in Morocco are under twenty-five years old and 29 per cent are under fifteen. One of the ominous gifts of modernization, child labour, is due to many factors, but mainly the disintegration of the traditional rural social structure, coupled with the rapid increase in population.

Apart from civil servants and maids, women's participation in the economy is concentrated in four kinds of activities: agriculture, cattle-raising, and the textile and ready-made clothes industries.

But since official documents define 'economically active' so that it includes both people holding jobs and those looking for jobs, a thorough picture of the female labour situation cannot be drawn without looking at female unemployment. According to the official data, the number of people employed has not risen since 1960, but the structure of unemployment by sex has registered a spectacular change. While the number of unemployed males remained unchanged, the number of women seeking jobs increased tenfold in eleven years. While female unemployment accounted for less than 2% of the total unemployment figure in 1960, it reached 21% in 1971. The absence of an institutionalized right to work predisposes women to fall prey to unemployment much more easily than their male colleagues. In the cities the rate of activity and the level of unemployment are higher for women than for men.[22]

The 1971 census defines women working within the household as inactive. Some 2,800,000 Moroccan housewives are considered to contribute nothing to society. And, as the census-takers admit, 'in rural areas women's participation in economic activity is confused with housework, and a certain reticence on the part of the husband to declare his wife active was noticed.'[23] In 1960 the number of women whose labour was under-reported was estimated to be 1,200,000. A more accurate census would have inflated the number of unemployed people tremendously by adding the 'under-estimated' female farm-workers.

Let us now return to the ideological implications of this massive access of women to the job market. The traditional definition of femininity might be reassuring in some respects. The number of unemployed women, for example, is less important than the number of unemployed men because after all the woman's place is in the home and her husband guarantees her needs, her *nafaqa*. Since women's right to work outside the home is still ambiguous, and since the provisions of the

160

Muduwana are clear, the state is obliged to create jobs for men only. To supply jobs for women is therefore not an obligation but an act of benevolent generosity. To keep women in the home, under the control of men, satisfies needs both psychological and economic in a Third World country in which the economy is in deep crisis and is strongly dependent. If the Muslim family, with its territorial sexuality, did not exist, it would have been created. It is thus not difficult to understand the utility of the various conservative arguments advising women to return to the hearths their grandmothers occupied.

Functions of Sexual Repression
in a Depressed Economy

Less visible but probably more pernicious than the economic aspect is the psychological function of female oppression as an outlet for male frustration and aggression. Wilhelm Reich drew attention to the functions of the patriarchal family in economically depressed societies. He emphasized that 'economic freedom goes hand in hand with the dissolution of old institutions', particularly those 'governing sexual policies',[24] and that sexually frustrated males are less likely to rebel against economic exploitation.

> The suppression of one's primitive material needs compasses a different result than the suppression of one's sexual needs. The former incites to rebellion, whereas the latter—inasmuch as it causes sexual needs to be repressed —withdraws them from consciousness and anchors itself as a moral defence, prevents rebellion against both forms of suppression. Indeed the inhibition of rebellion itself is unconscious. In the consciousness of the average non-political man there is not even a trace of it.[25]

A sexually repressed male is preoccupied with symbols such as 'purity' and 'honour' because his experience of genital sexuality is 'dirty' by his society's standards and, consequently, by his own standards. For example, the rural Moroccan youth whose sexual desires are savagely separated from their female goals so that he has to choose between sodomy, homosexuality, and masturbation (all equally condemned) is likely to be particularly sensitive to the ideas of honour and purity.

> The man who attains genital satisfaction is honourable, responsible, brave, and controlled without making much of a fuss about it. These attitudes are an organic part of his personality. The man whose genitals are weakened, whose sexual structure is full of contradictions, must continually remind himself to control his sexuality, to preserve his sexual dignity, to be brave in the face of temptations, etc.[26]

Honour and purity, two particularly sensitive emotional concepts in Muslim North African society, link the man's prestige in an almost fatal way to the sexual behaviour of the women under his charge, be they his wives, sisters, or unmarried female relatives.[27] A man who has a wife or sister working in an office or going to school is a man who runs a very serious chance of seeing 'his honour soiled'. He must face the real possibility of suffering the complete collapse of his prestige when one of his women is seen 'driving around with the boy next door' after school or office hours. To have men's honour embodied in women's sexual behaviour was a much safer system when women's space was strictly confined to the courtyard and ritual visits to the *hammam* or the local saint's tomb. It is no wonder that women who have such tremendous power to maintain or destroy a man's position in society are going to be the focus of his frustrations and aggression.

Male frustration is likely to be aggravated by the differences in the ways men and women are socialized to handle sexual drives. Men are encouraged to expect full satisfaction of their sexual desires, and to perceive their masculine identity as closely linked to that satisfaction. From an early age women are taught to curb their sexual drives. Little girls are told in detail about the vagina and the uterus, and about the penis's 'destructive' effects on these two parts of women's bodies. The *hammam*, where children bathe together with adults, is a normal place for questions and answers about human anatomy. A brother's circumcision at the age of five is also an occasion for little girls to ask questions. Moreover, grown-ups frequently do not wait until the child asks. They volunteer the information upon which the honour and prestige of the group depend. (As a child I was constantly warned about the implications of my sexual behaviour, and on the occasion of my first period I was treated to a long conference with my mother and oldest aunt. A horde of cousins were set on my trail, assigned to observe my every move between Bab al-Hadid College and the house where I lived.)

The male child is introduced to sex differently. His penis, *htewta* ('little penis'), is the object of a veritable cult on the part of the women rearing him. Little sisters, aunts, maids, and mothers often attract the little boy's attention to his *htewta* and try to teach him to pronounce the word, which is quite a task given the gutteral initial letter *h*. One of the common games played by adult females with a male child is to get him to understand the connection between *sidi* (master) and the *htewta*. *Hada sidhum* ('This is their master'), say the women, pointing to the child's penis. They try to make him repeat the sentence while pointing to his own penis. The kissing of the child's penis is a normal gesture for a female relative who has not seen him since his birth. *Tbarkallah 'ala-r-Rajal* ('God protect the man'), she may whisper. The child's phallic pride is enhanced systematically, beginning in the first years of life. And as a boy matures, the fact that men have privileges such as polygamy and repudiation, which allow them not only to have multiple sexual partners but also to change partners at will, gives him the impression that society is organized to satisfy his sexual wishes.

The young man is then confronted with the hard reality of adolescence, when sexual deprivation is systematically organized. He finds that he cannot have a woman if he does not pay the bride-price, a sum he often cannot afford until his mid-twenties, if he's lucky. If he wants to satisfy his sexual needs, he must break the law and have illicit intercourse. He is likely to be very upset by sexual restrictions he was not told about early enough. In fact, the sexual tragedy, often seen as a female problem, is an equally destructive masculine tragedy, as is clear in the unbelievable sexual misery of many of the heroes of Moroccan literature and plays.

The unexpected frustration that society imposes on the sexual desires of its young men is allowed no outward expression. Aggression against the managers of the Moroccan economy is violently discouraged and legally repressed. Anger at society turns in towards the family and women—objects of frustrated desire.[28] The family offers the sexually and politically oppressed Moroccan male a natural outlet for his frustrations.

> A person who fears to express his aggression directly against the original social objects responsible for his frustration may express his aggression instead against some other objects. . . . The tendency to express aggression against irrelevant objects would increase with increasing anxiety about expressing aggression against the actual source of frustration.[29]

A man who is both economically and sexually oppressed by his society is likely to find it less traumatizing to express his rage and resentment against his family than against his boss. And society encourages him to do so. It encourages the male to believe that his honour depends primarily on maintaining an iron grip on his women and children. As Reich says, 'sexual inhibition changes the structure of the economically oppressed in such a way that he acts, feels and thinks contrary to his own material interests.'[30] The tragedy of the Moroccan youth who wants to love a woman is that his actions are likely to be directly opposite to his desires. Society's conditioning—starting with his relationship with his mother[31] and including pressure on him to be 'a real man' and his legal right to demand the subordination of his wife—is likely to produce reflexes that pertain more to hatred than love.

The traditional order, empowered by the codification of the *shari'a* in the modern family code, views men and women as antagonists and dooms the conjugal unit to conflict. By affirming the man's right to have authority over women he can no longer control, given the breakdown of traditional spatial and economic structures, the modern *Code* places the man in a humiliating situation in which he perceives sexual desegregation and its effects as emasculating, given the difficulties he faces in fulfilling his traditional male role. For example, the rate of unemployment makes it difficult for the Moroccan male to perform the traditional duty of providing for his family. At the same time, allowing his wife to work outside, under the supervision of other males, makes him see himself, according to his traditional images of masculinity, as nothing more than a pimp (*qawwad*) or a cuckold (*qarran*).[32]

Male-female dynamics are influenced by two kinds of pressure:

1.   The need, emerging from the process of desegregation, to value the heterosexual relationship and to expect love and sex in the conjugal unit.
2.   The pressures from the prevailing traditional patterns, symbolized by parental authority and enhanced by modern family laws, to condemn the conjugal unit and debase sexual love.

The heterosexual relationship is caught between the poles of attraction and repulsion latent in traditional Muslim ideology. Modernization and economic necessity are breaking down the seclusion of women, which was the traditional Muslim solution to the conflict. Sexual desegregation creates new tensions and anxieties. Spatial boundaries and lines of authority between the sexes have become unclear, demanding completely new and often painful adjustments from both men and women. Nevertheless, despite the difficulties and tensions, despite the painful confrontations now being suffered by men and women in Morocco, a new phenomenon is now emerging: the conjugal couple made up of one man and one woman (without mamma). It is now slowly gaining in legitimacy. The women I interviewed back in 1971—regardless of social class, level of education, and activity—laid claim to the egalitarian couple, based on solidarity, as the foundation of a healthy family and a unique opportunity to raise generations of more fulfilled individuals, both emotionally and intellectually.

Conclusion
Women's Liberation
in Muslim Countries

People tend to perceive women's liberation as a spiritual and not a material problem. We have seen this to be true in the case of Islam, where changes in conditions for women were perceived by Muslim male literature as involving solely religious problems. Muslims argued that changes in women's conditions were a direct attack on Allah's realm and order. But changes in the twentieth century, mainly in socialist societies, have showed that the liberation of women is predominantly an economic issue. Liberation is a costly affair for any society, and women's liberation is primarily a question of the allocation of resources. A society that decides to liberate women not only has to provide them with jobs, but also has to take upon itself the responsibility for providing child care and food for all workers regardless of sex. A system of kindergartens and canteens is an indispensable investment promoting the liberation of women from traditional domestic chains.

The capacity to invest in women's liberation is not a function of a society's wealth, but of its goals and objectives. A society whose ultimate goal is profit rather than the development of human potential proves reluctant and finally unable to afford a state system of child-care centres and canteens. Mariarosa Della Costa explains how capitalism maintains, in the midst of its modern management of human resources and services, a pre-capitalist army of wageless workers—housewives—who provide unpaid child-care and domestic services.[1] Hence the paradox: the 'richest' nation in the world (the nation that controls most of the world's resources), the United States, is unable in spite of its much publicized abundance to afford a system of free kindergartens and canteens to promote women's humanhood.

Have Arab societies taken a stand on the question? Until now, they have had no effective systematic and coherent programme. In the absence of such programmes, and because it is too soon to judge the emerging trends concerning the liberation of women in independent Arab-Muslim states, I will limit myself to a few speculative remarks on the likely future of women in the Arab world. Before going any further, I want to draw attention to the inadequacy of the only two models for 'women's liberation' presently available in the Arab-Muslim world.

The scarcity of effective models for 'liberated women' might explain the particularly strong reaction that 'women's liberation' evokes from most Muslims. (By effective models I mean models which evoke images specific enough to stir people's emotions.) One of these is an intrinsic Arab model, that of pre-Islamic family and sexuality patterns, the other is exogenous, the Western model. The socialist models of sexuality and family patterns are hardly known and enjoy a carefully cultivated indifference, based more often on ignorance than on knowledgeable analysis. Both the pre-Islamic and Western models provoke traumatizing images of sexuality, although for different reasons.

Pre-Islamic sexuality is described in Arab literature as a chaotic, all-embracing, rampant promiscuity whose essence is women's self-determination, freedom to choose and dimiss their sexual partner, or partners, and the utter unimportance of the biological father and paternal legitimacy. The idea of female sexual self-determination which is suggested by the term 'women's liberation' is likely to stir ancestral fears of this mythical (pre-civilized) *jahiliya* woman before whom the male is deprived of all his initiative, control, and privilege. The way to win over a 'liberated woman' is to please her and make her love you, not to coerce and threaten her. But Muslim society does not socialize men to win women through love; they are badly equipped to deal with a self-determined woman; hence the repulsion and fear that accompany the idea of women's liberation.

Confusing sexual self-determination of women with chaotic, lawless animalistic promiscuity is not exclusive to Muslim societies facing drastic changes in their family structure. This confusion existed and still exists in any society whose family system is based on the enslavement of the woman. Marx and Engels had to attack repeatedly the confusion of bourgeois writers which distorted their thinking about any family in which the woman was not reduced to an acquiescent slave.[2] They had to show again and again that a non-bourgeois sexuality based on equality of the sexes does not necessarily lead to promiscuity, and that the bourgeois family pattern was an unjustified dehumanization of half of society. The same argument holds for Muslim societies. Muslim marriage is based on the premisses that social order can be maintained only if women's dangerous potential for chaos is restrained by a dominating non-loving husband who has, besides his wife, other females (concubines, co-wives, and prostitutes) available for his sexual pleasure under equally degrading conditions.[3] A new sexual order based on the absence of dehumanizing limitations of women's potential means the destruction of the traditional Muslim family. In this respect, fears associated with changes in the family and the condition of women are justified. These fears, embedded in the culture through centuries of women's oppression, are echoed and nourished by the vivid, equally degrading images of Western sexuality and its disintegrating family patterns portrayed on every imported television set.

It is understandable that Muslim fathers and husbands feel horrified at the idea of their own family and sexuality patterns being transformed into Western patterns. The striking characteristic of Western sexuality is the mutilation of the woman's integrity, her reduction to a few inches of nude flesh whose shades and forms are photographed *ad infinitum* with no goal other than profit. While Muslim exploitation of the female is cloaked under veils and hidden behind walls, Western exploitation has the bad taste of being bare and over-exposed.

It is worth noting that the fears of Muslim fathers and husbands are not totally unfounded; the nascent 'liberation' of Muslim women has indeed borrowed many characteristics of Western women's way of life. The first gesture of 'liberated' Arab women was to discard the veil for Western dress, which in the thirties, forties, and fifties was that of the wife of the colonizer. Speaking a foreign language was often a corollary to discarding the veil, the first 'liberated' women usually being members of the upper and middle classes. And here we touch upon another aspect of the difficulty Muslim societies have in adjusting to female self-determination. The Westernization of the first 'liberated' women was and still is part and parcel of the Westernization of the Arab-Muslim ruling classes. The fears awakened by the Westernization of women can be interpreted as simply another instance of Muslim society believing that males are able to select what is good in Western civilization and discard bad elements, while women are unable to choose correctly. This is concordant with the classical Muslim view of women as being unable to judge what is good and what is bad.

Another factor that helps in understanding men's fears of the changes now taking place is that Westernization of women has enhanced their seductive powers. We have seen that the Muslim ethic is against women's ornamenting themselves and exposing their charms; veil and walls were particularly effective anti-seduction devices. Westernization allowed ornamented and seductively clad female bodies to appear on the streets. It is interesting that while Western women's liberation movements had to repudiate the body in pornographic mass media, Muslim women are likely to claim the right to their bodies as part of their liberation movement. Previously a Muslim woman's body belonged to the man who possessed her, father or husband. The mushrooming of beauty salons and ready-to-wear boutiques in Moroccan towns can be interpreted as a forerunner of women's urge to claim their own bodies, which will culminate in more radical claims, such as the claim to birth control and abortion.

Having described the available models and their negative reception, let me hazard a few speculations on the future of women's liberation in Muslim societies, based on a projection from the current situation.

It is hardly contestable that there have been substantial changes in Muslim women's condition. Women have gained many rights that were denied them before, such as the right to education, the right to vote and be elected, and the right to use non-domestic spaces. But an important characteristic of this nascent 'liberation' is that it is not the outcome of a careful plan of controlled nation-wide development. Neither is it the outcome of the massive involvement of women in labour markets, coupled with organized women's movements. The partial, fragmented acquisition of rights by women in Arab-Muslim countries is a random, non-planned, non-systematic phenomenon, due mainly to the disintegration of the traditional system under pressures from within and without. Muslim women's liberation is therefore likely to follow a *sui generis* pattern.

To the dismay of rigid conservatives desperately preoccupied with static tradition, change is shaking the foundations of the Muslim world. Change is multidimensional and hard to control, especially for those who deny it. Whether accepted or rejected, change gnaws continuously at the intricate mechanisms of social life, and the more it is thwarted, the deeper and more surprising are its implications. The heterosexual unit is not yet officially admitted by Muslim rulers to be a crucial focus of the process of national development. Development plans devote hundreds of pages to the mechanization of agriculture, mining, and banking, and only a few pages to the family and women's condition. I want to emphasize on the one hand the deep and far-reaching processes of change at work in the Muslim family, and on the other hand the decisive role of women and the family in any serious development plan in the Third World economy.

The Family and Women

As shown earlier, one of the distinctive characteristics of Muslim sexuality is its territoriality, which reflects a specific division of labour and a specific conception of society and power. The territoriality of Muslim sexuality sets patterns of ranks, tasks, and authority. Spatially confined, women were taken care of materially by the men who possessed them, in exchange for total obedience and sexual and reproductive services. The whole system was organized so that the Muslim *umma* was actually a society of male citizens who possessed, among other things, the female half of the population. In his introduction to *Women and Socialism*, George Tarabishi remarks that people generally say that there are one hundred million Arabs, but in fact there are only fifty million, the female population being prevented from taking part in social responsibilities.[4] Muslim men have always had many more rights and privileges than Muslim women, including even the right to kill their women. (The Moroccan penal code still shows a trace of this power in Article 418, which grants extenuating circumstances to a man who kills his adulterous wife.[5]) Men imposed on women an artificially narrow existence both physically and spiritually.

This territoriality (the confining of women) is in the process of being dismantled, modernization having triggered mechanisms of socio-economic change that no group is able to control. Philip Slater, in his studies of societies based on sex-antagonisms, came to the conclusion that such systems are manageable only 'under conditions of strong ties and residential stability'.[6] Morocco's family structure and tradition of residential stability are disintegrating with the increase of individual salaries and the breakdown of the corporate family system, at least in the urban middle class. The majority of traditional women interviewed lived with their husbands' parents at the beginning of their married lives. Then, for 'no reason', that is, with no open hostility, the extended family broke up. In two cases, the reason advanced was quarrelling between son and uncle. But a century ago quarrels did not break up Moroccan families. A more likely reason is the ability of the son to earn an adequate salary independent of his father and uncle. Having his own income, he is now able to break away. The fact that the state, the most important employer, requires a certain mobility from its civil servants is an important element in the destruction of the old family structure. Unnecessary confusion and anxiety stem from the fact that the government supports the traditional ideology and enforces it as law, while its economic plans and programmes promote a different reality. The new reality is shaking the traditional structure, increasing role confusion and conflicts, and bringing greater suffering for the individuals involved, regardless of sex.

One of the results of the break-up of traditional family life is that, for the first time in the history of modern Morocco, the husband is facing his wife directly. Men and women live more closely and interact more than they ever did before, partly because of the decline of anti-heterosexual factors such as the mother-in-law's presence and sexual segregation. This direct confrontation between men and women brought up in sexually antagonistic traditions is likely to be laden with tensions and fears on both sides.

The future of male-female dynamics greatly depends on the way modern states handle the readjustment of sexual rights and the reassessment of sexual status. In Morocco the legislature has retained the traditional concept of marriage. The ancient definition of sex statuses based on division of labour according to sex was reenacted as the basis of family law: Article 35 defines the man as the sole provider for the family. He is responsible not only for himself but also for his able-bodied wife, who is consequently defined as economically dependent, her participation being limited to sexual services, reproduction, and housework.

To define masculinity as the capacity to earn a salary is to condemn those men suffering from unemployment (or the threat of it) to perceive economic problems as castration threats. Moreover, since the *Code* defines earning a salary as a man's role, a woman who earns a salary will be perceived as either masculine or castrating. If the privileges of men become more easily accessible to women, then men will be perceived as becoming more feminine.

By emphasizing the link between masculinity and economic success for men, the Moroccan *Code* reactivates traditional patterns of self-esteem whereby a man's prestige depends on his wealth, at the very moment when economic problems are making it difficult for a growing majority of Moroccans to amass wealth. The authority of males, traditionally embodied in their ability to provide for their families, is seriously jeopardized by their present situation. Moroccan males now have great difficulty achieving traditional masculine recognition:

> There is no power but in men
> There are no men without money.[7]

Modernization, in these terms, clearly appears to be a castrating phenomenon. By emphasizing the traditional definitions of masculinity, the state encourages ambivalent feelings in men, both toward the inactive women for whom they cannot provide and toward the active ones they experience as castrators. The ambivalence aggravates the traditional fears of devouring females latent in all patriarchal cultures. The Moroccan male is increasingly encouraged to look upon himself not as a multi-dimensional person, but primarily as a sexual agent, and it is from sex that he is encouraged to expect gratification, prestige, and power. Moroccans are allowed to boss their wives and children, but if they dare to raise objections to economic and political conditions, their initiatives are severely discouraged and often violently repressed. The complementarity of an authoritarian political structure and the authoritarian power of the husband and father seems to be a feature of transitional societies unable to create an effective development programme to face change with effective planning. In Morocco the events of the past decades have brought about a serious erosion of male supremacy which is generating greater tension between the sexes, at least in this transitional period. Surprisingly enough, the serious blows to male supremacy did not come from women, who have been reduced to helplessness by their historical situation, but from the state.

The State as the Main Threat to Traditional Male Supremacy

In spite of its continuous support for traditional male rights, the state constitutes a threat and a mighty rival to the male as both father and husband. The state is taking over the traditional functions of the male head of the family, such as education and the provision of economic security for members of the household. By providing a nation-wide state school system and an individual salary for working wives, daughters, and sons, the state has destroyed two pillars of the father's authority. The increasingly preeminent role of the state has stripped the traditionally powerful family head of his privileges and placed him in a subordinate position with respect to the state not very different from the position of women in the traditional family. The head of the family is dependent on the state (the main employer) to provide for him just as women are dependent on their husbands in traditional settings. Economic support is given in exchange for obedience, and this tends to augment male-female solidarity as a defence against the state and its daily frustrations.

The word 'sexist' as it is currently employed in English has the connotation that males are favoured at the expense of females. It is my belief that, in spite of appearances, the Muslim system does not favour men; the self-fulfilment of men is just as impaired and limited as that of women. Though this equality of oppression is concealed by the world-renowned 'privileges' of the Muslim male, I have tried to illustrate it by showing how polygamy and repudiation are oppressive devices for both sexes. The Muslim theory of sexuality views women as fatally attractive and the source of many delights. Any restrictions on the man's right to such delights, even if they take the form of restrictions on women alone (seclusion, for example), are really attacks on the male's potential for sexual fulfilment.

It might well be argued that the Muslim system makes men pay a higher psychological price for the satisfaction of sexual needs than women, precisely because women are conditioned to accept sexual restrictions as 'natural', while men are encouraged to expect a thorough satisfaction of their sexual needs. Men and women are socialized to deal with sexual frustration differently. We know that an individual's discontent grows as his expectations rise. From the age of four or earlier, a woman in Moroccan society is made aware of the sexual restrictions she has to face. The difficulties a Moroccan male experiences in dealing with sexual frustration are almost unknown to the Moroccan woman, who is traumatized early enough to build adequate defences. In this sense also the Muslim order is not 'sexist'.

Future Trends

In the short run the reduced power of the head of the family produces tension in the family such that resentful males are likely to compensate by oppressing their wives and children. But in the long run, it is likely to generate increasing male-female rapprochement in the face of the common and increasingly similar preoccupations of their daily reality. It can lead, as it already has in the case of young couples, to greater collaboration between husband and wife and a strengthening of the conjugal unit in the face of the system's shortcomings.

We have seen that the only model for a conjugal unit available in a Muslim society dictates how men and women should relate to each other. The relation in a traditional family is a master-slave relation where love is excluded and condemned as a weakness on the part of men. The separation between love and sex is clearly illustrated by another model of male-female relatedness, this time taken not from institutions, but from literature: the model of Udrite love.[8] Udrite love is a variety of romantic love very important in Arab literature. It enjoys end-lessly renewed fame through the poems sung by the most famous Arab singers, broadcast by the mass media. The characteristic of the Udrite lover is that he never has sexual intercourse with his beloved, and since in Arab-Muslim society marriage is synonymous with blessed sexuality, the Udrite lovers never marry. Countless obstacles from within and with-out stand between them for ever, keeping their unsatisfied bodies burning with a 'spiritual' flame. For centuries this has been presented as the highest form of love, where the soul triumphs over the flesh, the spirit over the body, refinement and sophistication over animality (spirit, soul, refinement, and sophistication all being linked with the absence of sexual inter-course). The model of Udrite love is now being attacked as a sick way of loving a woman. It is quite revealing that the most vehement attacks on Udrite love have come from male writers, Sadiq Jalal al-Azm[9] and Tahar Labib Djedidi.[10] Both men— the first through a psychoanalytical, the second through a linguistic approach—come to similar conclusions. Tahar Djedidi argues that Udrite love is the expression of an eco-nomically and politically impotent community, the Banu Udra, who were deprived of their traditional tribal privileges with the growth of the centralized Muslim Empire.[11] For Jalal al-Azm, Udrite love, which implies that a man can love a woman only if he avoids sexual intercourse with her, is the distorted conception of love in a sexually oppressed society. Udrite love could exist only outside the conjugal unit; the wife, by definition, could never be the object of such love.

These recent analyses of Udrite love support my own conclusion, based on my analysis of traditional conjugal models, that modern Muslim societies have to face the fact that the traditional family mutilates women by depriving them of their humanity. What modern Muslim societies ought to strive toward is a family based on the unfragmented wholeness of the woman. Sex with an unfragmented human female is a glorious, not a soiling and degrading act. It implies and generates tenderness and love. Allegiance and involvement with an unfragmented woman do not distract men from their social duties, because the woman is not a marginal tabooed individual; rather, she is the centre, the source, the generator of order and life.

Islam's basically positive attitude toward sexuality is more conducive to healthy perspectives of a self-realizing sexuality, harmoniously integrated in social life, than the West's basically negative attitude toward sexuality. Serious changes in male-female conditioning in Western countries imply revolutionary changes in society which these reformist countries are determined to avoid at any cost. Muslim societies *cannot* afford to be reformist; they do not have sufficient resources to be able to offer palliatives. A superficial replastering of the system is not a possible solution for them.

At a deeper level than laws and official policy, the Muslim social order views the female as a potent aggressive individual whose power can, if not tamed and curbed, corrode the social order. It is very likely that in the long run such a view will facilitate women's integration into the networks of decision-making and power. One of the main obstacles Western women have been dealing with is their society's view of women as passive inferior beings. The fact that generations of university-educated women in both Europe and America failed to win access to decision-making posts is due in part to this deeply ingrained image of women as inferior. The Muslim image of women as a source of power is likely to make Muslim women set higher and broader goals than just equality with men. The most recent studies on the aspirations of both men and women seem to come to the same conclusion: the goal is not to achieve equality with men. Women have seen that what men have is not worth getting. Women's goals are already being phrased in terms of a global rejection of established sexual patterns, frustrating for males and degrading for females. This implies a revolutionary reorganization of the entire society, starting from its economic structure and ending with its grammar. Jalal al-Azm excuses himself at the beginning of the book for using the term 'he' throughout the book while in fact he should be using a neutral term, because his findings are valid for both men and women.[12] As a social scientist he resents being a prisoner of Arabic grammar, which imposes a sex-defined pronoun.[13] But not many Arab males yet feel ill-at-ease with sex-biased Arabic grammar, though a majority already feel indisposed by the economic situation.

The holders of power in Arab countries, regardless of their political make-up, are condemned to promote change, and they are aware of this, no matter how loud their claim to uphold the 'prestigious past' as the path to modernity. Historians have interpreted the somewhat cyclical resurgence of traditional rhetoric as a reflex of ruling groups threatened by acute and deep processes of change.[14] The problem Arab societies face is not whether or not to change, but how fast to change. The link between women's liberation and economic development is shown by the similarities in the conditions of the two sexes in the Third World; both sexes suffer from exploitation and deprivation. Men do not have, as in the so-called abundant Western societies, glaring advantages over women. Illiteracy and unemployment are suffered by males as well as females. This similarity of men and women as equally deprived and exploited individuals assumes enormous importance in the likely evolution of Third World family structure. George Tarabishi has pointed out the absurdity of men who argue that women should not be encouraged to get jobs in Arab society, where men suffer from unemployment.[15] He argues that society should not waste human resources in unemployment, but systematically channel the wealth of resources into productive tasks. The female half of human resources is more than welcome in the Arab future.

One may speculate that women's liberation in an Arab context is likely to take a faster and more radical path than in Western countries. Women in Western liberal democracies are organizing themselves to claim their rights, but their oppressors are strong, wealthy, and reformist regimes. The dialogue takes place within the reformist framework characteristic of bourgeois democracies. In such situations, serious changes are likely to take a long time. American women will get the right to abortion but it will be a long time before they can prevent the female's body from being exploited as a marketable product. Muslim women, on the contrary, engage in a silent but explosive dialogue with a fragile ruling class whose major task is to secure economic growth and plan a future without exploitation and deprivation. The Arab ruling classes are beginning to realize that they are charged with building a sovereign future, which necessarily revolves around the location and adequate utilization of all human and natural resources for the benefit of the entire population. The Arab woman is a central element in any sovereign future. Those who have not realized this fact are misleading themselves and their countries.

Notes

The version of the Koran used throughout this book is Mohammed Marmaduke Pickthall's *The Meaning of the Glorious Koran* (New York, New American Library, thirteenth printing). Abbreviations used in the notes are:

B for *bab* ('chapter');
H for *hadith* ('verbal tradition of Muhammad');
K for *kitab* ('book');
BESM for *Bulletin Economique et Social du Maroc*.

Preface

1. It is interesting that most of this literature is written by men. Muslim writers seem to perceive the 'woman question' as a problem between women and Islam, as is illustrated by the following titles (translated from the Arabic originals);

Said al-Afghani, *Islam and Women*, Damascus 1964;
Abd al-Qadir al-Qaramani, *Women From the Viewpoint of Islam*, Aleppo, n.d.;
Jafar al-Naqdi, *Islam and Women*;
Sadiq al-Qumaili, *Women's Personality in Islam*, Beirut 1972;
Muhammad al-Shayyal, *Women in Islam*, Cairo, n.d.;
Mahmud Shaltut, *Women in the Koran*, Cairo, 1963;
Abbas Mahmud al-Aqqad, *Women in the Koran*, Cairo, n.d.;
Abd al-Qadir al-Maghribi, *Muhammad and Women*, Beirut 1929;
Muhammad al-Mahdi al-Hajuwi, *Women: Shari'a and Law*, Casablanca 1967;
A. Afifi, *Arab Women: Jahiliya and Islam*, Cairo, n.d.

Apart from generally restating the position of women in Islam, this masculine literature focuses on another problem that men seem to feel is central:

Muhammad Nasr al-Din al-Albani, *The Seclusion of Muslim Women in the Book and the Sunna*, Beirut, n.d.;
Abu Radwan al-Sanusi, *Women: Seclusion and De-Seclusion*, Beirut, n.d.;
Abu'l-Ala al-Mawdudi, *Seclusion*, Damascus, n.d.;
Mustafa Naja, *Explanation of the Institution of Seclusion*, Beirut, n.d.

Introduction

1. *Code du Statut Personnel* (Personal Status Code), Dahir no. I-57-343, 22 November 1957, *Bulletin Officiel* no. 2378, 23 May 1958.

2. Malik Ibn Anas, *al-Muwatta*, Cairo, n.d.

3. Salama Musa, *Woman is Not the Plaything of Man*, Cairo 1955.

4. Ibid., p. 53. See also Abdallah Laroui, *L'idéologie arabe contemporaine*, Paris 1967, p. 51.

5. Salama Musa, *Woman Is Not the Plaything of Man*, p. 106.

6. Qasim Amin, *The Liberation of Women*, Cairo 1928, the edition published to commemorate the twentieth anniversary of the author's death, p. 18.

7. Ibid., p. 15.

8. Ibid., p. 16.

9. Ibid., p. 10.

10. Ibid., p. 9.

11. Ibn Murad al-Salah, *al-Hidad alq'l-mar'at al-hadad*, Tunis, n.d., p. 6.

12. Ibid., p. 70.

13. Daniel Lerner, *The Passing of Traditional Society, Modernizing of the Middle East*, New York 1958, p. 44.

14. Ibid., p. 47.

15. Anouar Abdel-Malek, *Egypt, Military Society*, New York 1968, p. 249.

16. Paul Coatalen, 'Ethnologie Barbare', in *Annales Marocaines de Sociologie*, 1970, pp. 3–11.

17. Allal al-Fasi, *The Independence Movements in Arab North Africa*, New York 1970, p. 381.

18. The first members of the Arab League were Egypt, Saudi Arabia, Iraq, Yemen, Syria, and Lebanon.

19. Allal al-Fasi, *Independence Movements in Arab North Africa*, p. 409.

20. Wilfred Cantwell-Smith, *The Meaning and End of Religion*, New York 1964, p. 79.

21. Montgomery Watt, *Muhammad at Medina*, Oxford 1956, p. 239.

22. H. A. R. Gibb, 'Constitutional Organization' in *Origin and Development of Islamic Law*, ed. M. Khaduri and H. J. Liebesny, Vol. I, Washington, D.C. 1955, p. 3.

23. Gertrude Stern, *Marriage in Early Islam*, London 1931, p. 71.

24. Joseph Schacht, *An Introduction to Islamic Law*, London 1964, p. 161.

25. In *The Muqaddimah, An Introduction to History*, translated from the Arabic by Franz Rosenthal, Princeton, N.J. 1969. The North African historian Ibn Khaldun (1332–1406) sketched a model of the Muslim social order. He was interested in analysing what was happening to the then disintegrating Muslim world, which had stood uncontested in the Mediterranean arena until a few centuries before. Although primarily concerned with an entirely different problem, the growth and death of civilization, Ibn Khaldun analysed the reasons the Muslims had succeeded for so long.

According to his theory, the survival of human groups requires the surrender of individual will to a set of social norms or laws. There are two kinds of social norms: those having a human basis, reason, and those having a supernatural basis, religion.

> If these norms are ordained by the intelligent leading personalities and minds of the dynasty, the result will be a political [institution] with an intellectual [rational] basis, if they are ordained by God through a lawgiver who establishes them as [religious] laws, the result will be a political [institution] with a religious basis. (*The Muqaddimah*, p. 154.)

A political institution having a religious basis is far superior to a political institution having a rational basis, not because of any deficiency in the latter's mechanisms, but because of the narrowness of its scope. Reason governs only this world's interests, while religious institutions govern both.

> Political laws consider only worldly interests. On the other hand, the intention the lawgiver has concerning mankind is their welfare in the other world, therefore it is necessary, as required by the religious law, to cause the mass to act in accordance with the religious laws in all their affairs touching both this world and the other world. (*The Muqaddimah*, p. 155.)

26. H. A. R. Gibb, 'Constitutional Organization', p. 3.

27. S. G. Vesey-Fitzgerald, 'Nature and Source of the *Sharia*', in *Origin and Development of Islamic Law*, p. 109.

28. Ibid., p. 104.

29. Ibid., p. 85.

30. J. Schacht, *Introduction to Islamic Law*, p. 76.

31. Ibid., p. 101.

32. Ibid., pp. 210–214.

33. Ibid., p. 100.

34. Abdallah Laroui, *L'Histoire du Maghreb, Un Essai de Synthèse*, Paris 1970, p. 346.

35. This opportunism is clearly illustrated in the economic options adopted by the Moroccan state during the years of independence. A revealing analysis of these options is Samir Amin's *Le Maghreb Moderne*, Paris 1970, chapter VI: 'Le Maroc, Hésitations et Contradictions'. Also A. Belal, 'L'Orientation des investissements et les impératifs du développement national', *BESM* XXVIII, p. 100; and T. Ben Cheikh, 'Planification et politique agricole', Part I, *BESM* XXXI, no. 112–113 (January–June 1969), pp. 191, 199, and Part II in *BESM* XXXI, no. 114 (July–September 1969), pp. 75–83.

36. Salama Musa, *Woman Is Not the Plaything of Man*, chapter entitled 'Our Philosophy on Women'.

37. Dahir, no. I-57-190, 19 August 1957, *Bulletin Officiel* no. 2341, 6 September 1957, p. 1163.

38. Sunni (that is, 'orthodox') Muslims recognize four legitimate schools of law:

Hanafi: The founder of the school was Abu Hanifa (699–769), who undertook to create precedents by analogy with the decisions of the first four caliphs; it holds sway mainly in central Asia, northern India, and among the Turks, but also in Pakistan, China, and Japan.

Shafii: The founder was Abu Abdullah Muhammad al-Shafi'i (770–819); centred mainly in lower Egypt, southern India, and Malaya.

Malekite: The founder was Malik Ibn Anas (705–795), whose teachings were confined to the traditions (*hadith*). The title of his major work, *al-Muwatta*, means 'the path'. The school holds sway mainly in Africa, especially north Africa, and upper Egypt.

Hanbalite: The founder was Abu Hanbal (780–855). This school is characterized by a strong puritanical tendency.

All four schools agree on the fundamental dogmas, but differ in the application of the Koran and its interpretation.

Chapter 1

1. Ibn Khaldun, *The Muqaddimah, An Introduction to History*, translated by Franz Rosenthal, Princeton, N.J. 1969, pp. 160–161.

2. Ibid., p. 161.

3. Ibid.

4. Abu Hamid al-Ghazali, *Ihya Ulum al-Din*, Cairo, n.d.

5. Ibid., p. 28.

6. Ibid., p. 25.

7. Ibid.

8. Ibid., p. 27.

9. George Peter Murdock, *Social Structure*, New York 1965, p. 273.

10. Ibid.

11. Qasim Amin, *The Liberation of Women*, Cairo 1928, p. 64.

12. Ibid., p. 65.

13. Al-Ghazali, *The Revivification of Religious Sciences*, vol. II, chapter on marriage; and Mizan al-'Amal, *Criteria for Action*, Cairo 1964.

14. Abbas Mahmud al-Aqqad, *Women in the Koran*, Cairo n.d.

15. Ibid., p. 7; the verse he refers to is verse 228 of sura 2, which is striking by its inconsistency. The whole verse reads as follows:

> And they [women] have rights similar to those [of men] over them in kindness, and men are a degree above them.

I am tempted to interpret the first part of the sentence as a simple stylistic device to bring out the hierarchical content of the second part.

16. Ibid., p. 24.

17. Ibid., p. 25. The biological assumption behind Aqqad's sweeping generalizations is obviously fallacious.

18. Ibid., p. 18.

19. Ibid., p. 26.

20. A. Schultz, 'The Problem of Social Reality', *Collected Papers*, vol. I, The Hague, n.d., p. 101.

21. Ralph Linton, *The Study of Man*, London 1936, p. 116.

22. A. Schultz, *Collected Papers*, p. 9.

23. Sigmund Freud, *New Introductory Lectures on Psychoanalysis*, College Edition, New York 1965, p. 114.

24. Ibid.

25. Sigmund Freud, *Three Contributions to the Theory of Sex*, 2nd ed., New York 1909, p. 77.

26. Sigmund Freud, *New Introductory Lectures*, p. 114.

27. Al-Ghazali, *Revivification of Religious Sciences*, p. 51.

28. Una Stannard, 'Adam's Rib or the Woman Within', *Transaction*, November-December 1970, vol. 8, special issue on American Women, pp. 24–36.

29. Al-Ghazali, *Revivification*, p. 50. Not only is the woman granted ejaculation, she is also granted the capacity to have nocturnal ejaculation and 'sees what the man sees in sleep'. (Ibn Saad, *Kitab al-Tabaqat al-Kubra*, Beirut 1958, vol. 8, 'On Women', p. 858.)

30. Sigmund Freud, *Sexuality and the Psychology of Love*, New York 1963, pp. 196–197.

31. Ibid., p. 190.

32. Sigmund Freud, *Three Contributions*, p. 78.

33. Ibid.

34. Ibid.
35. Sigmund Freud, *New Introductory Lectures*, p. 132.
36. Al-Ghazali, *Revivification*, p. 50.
37. Ibid.
38. Ibid.
39. Sigmund Freud, *Three Contributions*, p. 14.
40. Ibid., p. 15.
41. Al-Ghazali, *Revivification*, p. 50.
42. Ibid.
43. Sigmund Freud, *New Introductory Lectures*, p. 116.
44. Abu Issa al-Tarmidi, *Sunan al-Tarmidi*, Medina n.d., vol. II, p. 413, B: 9, H: 1167.
45. Abu al-Hasan Muslim, *al-Jami' al-Sahih*, Beirut n.d., vol. III, Book of Marriage, p. 130.
46. Al-Tarmidi, *Sunan al-Tarmidi*, p. 419, B: 16, H: 1181. See also al-Bukhari, *Kitab al-Jami' al-Sahih*, Leyden, Holland 1868, vol. III, K: 67, B: 11.
47. Al-Tarmidi, *Sunan al-Tarmidi*, p. 419, B: 17. H: 1172.
48. Edward Westermark, *The Belief in Spirits in Morocco*, Abo, Finland 1920.
49. Edward Westermark, *Wit and Wisdom in Morocco: A Study of Native Proverbs*, London 1926, p. 330.
50. Sidi Abderahman al-Majdoub, *Les Quatrains du Mejdoub le Sarcastique, Poète Maghrébin du XVlième Siècle*, collected and translated by J. Scelles-Millie and B. Khelifa, Paris 1966, p. 161.
51. Ibid., p. 160.
52. Abu Abdallah Muhammad Ibn Ismail al-Bukhari, *Kitab al-Jami' al-Sahih*, Leyden, Holland 1868, p. 419, K: 67, B: 18.
53. Al-Ghazali, *Revivification*, p. 28.
54. Sigmund Freud, *Civilization and Its Discontents*, New York 1962.
55. Sigmund Freud, *A General Introduction to Psychoanalysis*, New York 1952, p. 27.
56. Al-Ghazali, *Revivification*, p. 32.

Chapter 2

1. Ignaz Goldziher, *Muslim Studies*, Chicago 1967, 'What is Meant by al-Jahiliya', p. 201.
2. Abu Abdallah Muhammad Ibn Ismail al-Bukhari, *Kitab al-Jami' al-Sahih*, p. 428, K: 67, B: 31.
3. In *al-Hayat al-Jinsiya Inda al-Arab* (*The Sexual Life of the Arabs*), Beirut 1958, Dr. Salah al-Din al-Munajid tries to show that Islam did not impose any restrictions on the sexual indulgence which prevailed during the *jahiliya*. According to him, Islam only codified and regularized the previous sexual practices. It seems obvious to me that Dr. Munajid must be thinking of male sexuality only.
4. Abu Hamid al-Ghazali, *The Revivification of Religious Sciences*, p. 30.
5. Edward Westermark, *Wit and Wisdom in Morocco, A Study of Native Proverbs*, p. 329.
6. Al-Ghazali, *Revivification*, p. 30.
7. Ibid.
8. Koran, sura 2: 231.
9. Al-Bukhari, *al-Jami' al-Sahih*, p. 426, K: 67, B: 35.
10. Ibn Hisham ed., *Sirat al-Nabi*, written by Ibn Ishaq, Cairo 1963, p. 121. All

Muhammad's male children died in infancy, creating a thorny problem for the fledgling *umma*: succession. The community, supposedly united, was divided by dissension and violence over the issue.

11. Ibn Saad, *Kitab al-Tabaqat al-Kubra*, vol. 8, 'On Women', Beirut 1958, pp. 154 and 150.

12. Ibid., p. 201.

13. Ibid., p. 141.

14. Ibid., p. 145.

15. Ibid., p. 141 and p. 148.

16. Ibid., p. 145.

17. Al-Bukhari, *al-Jami' al-Sahih*, p. 459, K: 68, B: 3.

18. Ibn Saad, *al-Tabaqat*, pp. 145, 148.

19. Al-Bukhari, *al-Jami' al-Sahih*, p. 459, K: 68, B: 3.

20. Abu Issa al-Tarmidi, *Sunan al-Tarmidi*, Medina n.d., p. 275, B: 4, H: 1092.

21. Ibn Saad, *al-Tabaqat*, pp. 120–123.

22. Ibid., p. 129.

23. Ibid., p. 212.

24. Ibid., p. 213.

25. Koran, sura 66, 3.

26. Ibn Saad, *al-Tabaqat*, p. 212.

27. Ibid., p. 117.

28. Ibid.

29. Ibid., p. 153.

30. Ibid., p. 101.

31. Koran, sura 33, 37.

32. Al-Tarmidi, *Sunan al-Tarmidi*, p. 404, B: 40, H: 1149. See also al-Ghazali, *Revivification*, p. 48. On the Prophet's involvement with his youngest wife, Aishah, see Nabia Abbott, *Aishah, the Beloved of Mohammed*, Chicago 1942.

33. J. Schacht, *Introduction to Islamic Law*, p. 125; also Malik, *al-Muwatta*, p. 11. In Muhammad's time the punishment was immurement:

> As for those of your women who are guilty of lewdness, call to witness four of you against them. And if they testify [to the truth of the allegation] then confine them to the house until death takes them or [until] Allah appoint
> for them a way [through new legislation]. (Koran, sura 4: 15.)

A new Muslim Law was revealed in sura 24: 2–10, which changed the punishment to scourging:

> The adulterer and the adulteress scourge each one of them a hundred stripes.

34. *Encyclopedia of Islam*, first edition, Leyden, Holland 1934, 'zina'.

35. Koran, sura 60: 12. It is important to understand the consensus under which women swore allegiance to Islam. Hind Bint Utba, an aristocratic Meccan woman, is reported to have reacted thus:

> The Prophet: And you will not commit *zina*?
> Hind: And does a free woman commit *zina*?
> The Prophet: And you will not kill your children [a reference to female infanticide]?
> Hind: And did you spare the life of any of our children? You killed all of

them yourself at Badr [a reference to the Battle of Badr, where the Muslims attacked Muhammad's own tribe] (Ibn Saad, *al-Tabaqat*, p. 9).

Hind's answer concerning *zina*, although startling, is quite enigmatic. It can mean either that Hind thought that *zina* was a debasing act which she, as a noble woman, would not engage in, or it could mean, on the contrary, that Hind thought that, as a freeborn woman, no sexual union she engaged in could be debasing. The Muslim interpretation would be the first one. Gertrude Stern inclines towards the second possibility (*Marriage in Early Islam*, London 1939, p. 9).

Hind does not seem to be a particularly zealous Muslim who was ready to accept the new creed unconditionally and uncritically. Her opinion about the Prophet seems to be critical, as her answer concerning the killing of children shows. She contested the Prophet's right to ask her not to kill her unwanted babies because, as the leader of the Muslims, he had made war on his own tribe and so in effect killed his own relatives.

36. Koran, sura 24: 32; also al-Bukhari, *al-Sahih*, pp. 410–411, K: 67, B: 1,2,3; also Muslim, *al-Jami' al-Sahih*, pp. 128, 129, 130; and finally al-Ghazali, *Revivification*, p. 22.

37. Gertrude Stern, *Marriage in Early Islam*, p. 94.

38. Al-Bukhari, *al-Jami' al-Sahih*, p. 445; K: 67, B: 85.

39. Koran, sura 2: 222.

40. Al-Ghazali, *Revivification*, p. 50.

41. Malik, *al-Muwatta*, p. 33.

42. Article 154, *Code du Statut Personnel*.

43. Malik, *al-Muwatta*, p. 19. Also Koran, sura 4: 34; and al-Bukhari, *al-Jami' al-Sahih*, p. 447, K: 67, B: 93.

44. Malik, *al-Muwatta*, p. 19.

45. Ibid.

46. Article 152, *Code du Statut Personnel*.

47. Malik, *al-Muwatta*, p. 23.

48. J. Schacht, *Islamic Law*, p. 164.

49. Malik, *al-Muwatta*, p. 23.

50. Montgomery Watt, *Muhammad at Medina*, pp. 273–274.

51. Al-Tarmidi, *Sunan al-Tarmidi*, p. 339; B: 33, H: 1140.

52. Koran, sura 65: 4.

53. Koran, sura 2: 226, 228, 234.

54. There was no *idda* for divorced women in pre-Islamic Arabia; only widows had to wait a year before re-marrying. See Ibn Habib al-Baghdadi, *al-Muhabbar*, p. 338. He states that there was insufficient space to name all the children born in the homes of second husbands and considered as belonging to them even though the first husband was the biological father.

55. Koran, sura 65: 4.

56. Malik, *al-Muwatta*, p. 30.

Chapter 3

1. Salah Ahmad al-'Ali, *Muhadarat fi'l-Tarikh al-'Arab*, Baghdad 1960, vol. 1, p. 136.

2. Ibid., p. 141.

3. Ibn Saad, *Kitab al-Tabaqat al-Kubra*, Beirut 1958, vol. 8.
4. Gertrude Stern, *Marriage in Early Islam*, London 1939.
5. Ibid., p. 70.
6. Ibid., p. 73.
7. Ibid., p. 62.
8. Ibid., p. 66.
9. Abi Jafar Muhammad Ibn Habib al-Baghdadi, *al-Muhabbar*, Beirut, pp. 310 ff. Arab men seem to have been against virilocality.
10. Ibn Hisham, ed., *Sirat al-Nabi*, written by Ibn Ishaq, Cairo 1963, vol. I, p. 89. Also Ibn Saad, *al-Tabaqat*, vol. I, p. 79.
11. Ibn Hisham, *Sirat*, p. 89.
12. Ibn Habib al-Baghdadi, *al-Muhabbar*, p. 398.
13. Ibn Saad, *al-Tabaqat*, vol. 8, p. 95.
14. Ibid., pp. 100, 118.
15. The case of Sakina Bint al-Hussein, the Prophet's granddaughter, is revealing. She married often and left the husbands she did not like. See al-Baghdadi, *al-Muhabbar*, p. 438.
16. Al-Bukhari, *al-Jami' al-Sahih*, p. 453, K: 67, B: 109.
17. Ibn Saad, *al-Tabaqat*, p. 337.
18. Ibid., p. 130.
19. Abu al-Faraj al-Isfahani, *Kitab al-Aghani*, Beirut 1909, vol. XVI, p. 102.
20. Ibid., p. 93.
21. Sir John Glubb, *A Short History of the Arab Peoples*, New York 1970, p. 43.
22. Muhammad Ibn Habib al-Baghdadi, Hyderabad 1942.
23. The translation is by A. F. L. Beeston, from his article 'The So-Called Harlots of Hadramaut', *Oriens* V, 1952, p. 16.
24. Ibid., p. 18.
25. Ibid., p. 20.
26. Ibid.
27. W. Robertson Smith, *Kinship and Marriage in Early Arabia*, Boston 1903, p. 94.
28. Ibid., p. 92.
29. Ibid., p. 156.
30. Ibid., p. 172.
31. Ibid., p. 92.
32. Ibid., p. 121.
33. Al-Isfahani, *al-Aghani*. Translation by W. R. Smith in *Kinship in Early Arabia*, p. 80.
34. Al-Isfahani, *al-Aghani*, vol. 16, p. 80.
35. Al-Bukhari, *al-Jami' al-Sahih*, p. 428, K: 67, B: 36. The translation is from M. Watt's *Muhammad at Medina*, pp. 378–379.
36. Ibid., p. 423, K: 67, B: 31.
37. Al-Tarmidi, *Sunan al-Tarmidi*, p. 395, B: 27, H: 1130.
38. Muslim, *al-Jami' al-Sahih*, pp. 130–131.
39. The Muslim world is divided into two camps: the Sunnis and the Shiites. The Sunnis, or orthodox, are so called because they follow the *sunna*, traditions having authority concurrent to and supplementary with the Koran. The Shiites are the partisans of the house of Ali, Muhammad's disciple, cousin, and son-in-law. They reject the authority of the *sunna* and believe that the sovereign Imamat ('the leadership of the faithful') is vested in Ali and his descendants, the sons of his wife Fatima (the Prophet's daughter). Consequently, they regard the

first three caliphs, Abu Bakr, Umar and Uthman, as usurpers. They are found chiefly in Iran and India, but their influence has penetrated other parts of the Muslim world.

40. W. R. Smith, *Kinship in Early Arabia*, p. 85.

41. Ibid., p. 94.

42. On the controversy concerning what constitutes the basic family unit, the trio mother-father-child or the duo mother-child, see the dialogue between R. Briffault and B. Malinowski in *Marriage, Past and Present*, Boston 1956, chapter III: 'What is a Family?' A humorous summary of the controversy is Robin Fox's *Kinship and Marriage*, New York 1967, chapter I: 'Kinship, Family and Descent'.

43. W. R. Smith, *Kinship in Early Arabia*, p. 177.

44. Ibid., p. 38.

45. Salama Musa, *Woman Is Not the Plaything of Man*, p. 20.

46. W. R. Smith, *Kinship in Early Arabia*, chapters II, IV, and V.

47. A. R. Radcliffe-Brown and Daryll Forde, *African Systems of Kinship and Marriage*, London 1950, p. 43.

48. M. Watt, *Muhammad at Medina*; and *Muhammad at Mecca*, London 1953.

49. M. Watt, *Muhammad at Medina*, p. 290.

50. Ibid., p. 261.

51. Ibid., p. 290 and p. 388.

52. This argument is a cliché used by traditionists and modernists alike. Qasim Amin argues in this sense when defending the position Islam granted women. A typical case of the use of the cliché is that of Muhammad al-Mahdi al-Hajawi in his book, *al-Mar'a bayna al-Shari'a wal-Qanun*, Casablanca, n.d.

53. Edouard Fares, *L'Honneur chez les arabes avant l'Islam: Etude de sociologie*, Paris 1932, p. 79.

54. M. Watt, *Muhammad at Medina*, p. 276.

55. Mohammed Marmaduke Pickthall, *The Meaning of the Glorious Koran*, introduction, p. 79.

56. M. Watt, *Muhammad at Medina*, p. 265.

57. Ibid., p. 145.

58. Ibid., p. 273.

59. Ibid., p. 271.

60. Al-Bukhari, *al-Jami' al-Sahih*, p. 440, K: 67, B: 81; also p. 447, K: 67, B: 90.

61. Samir Amin, *L'Economie arabe contemporaine*, Paris 1980, p. 16.

Chapter 5

1. P. Pascon and M. Bentahar, 'Ce que disent 269 Jeunes Ruraux', *BESM*, January-June 1969, XXI, pp. 112–113.

2. Ibid., p. 75.

3. *Population Légale*, Bureau of Statistics, Rabat, p. xii.

4. *Recensement Général de la Population et de l'Habitat*, 1971, vol. I, p. 5.

5. Pascon and Bentahar, '269 Jeunes Ruraux'. p. 63.

6. Ibid., p. 76.

7. Ibid.

8. Abdeljalil Agouram and Abdelaziz Belal, 'Bilan de l'économie marocaine depuis l'indépendance', *BESM* 33, no. 116, p. 11.

9. A new census was being conducted in the early eighties.

10. *Recensement Général*, 1971, vol. I, p. 9.

11. Pascon and Bentahar, '269 Jeunes Ruraux', p. 75.

12. Malika Belghiti, 'Les Relations féminines et le Statut de la Femme dans la famille rurale', *Collection du Bulletin Economique et Social du Maroc*, Rabat 1970, p. 24.

13. 'Enquête d'opinion sur la planification familiale en milieu urbain', Ministry of Public Health, Rabat 1966, p. 12.

14. *'Ahd* is a binding verbal promise. Edward Westermark gives a description of the *'ahd* mechanism in *Ritual and Belief in Morocco*, London 1926, vol. I, p. 564.

15. The Koran considers the sexual relationship between son-in-law and mother-in-law incestuous: sura 4: 23.

16. A basic description of the mechanism of the parent's curse is in E. Westermark, *Wit and Wisdom*.

17. Nine years after this research was done, the disintegration of rural society seems to have gone much further. Prostitution seems to have spread dramatically. In a society that considers itself Muslim, this is a sure sign of the sharpness of social conflict. Prostitution is a key phenomenon in that it expresses the coincidence of two basic elements of human life, economic and sexual.

Chapter 6

1. Al-Ghazali, *Revivification of Religious Sciences*, Cairo n.d., p. 39.

2. Ibid.

3. Koran, sura 78: 32.

4. Revulsion with sex itself is an idea alien to orthodox Islam. Ghazali is supposed to have written his *Revivification* during a mystical ascetic retreat between 1095 and 1105.

5. Al-Ghazali, 'Criterion for Action', Cairo 1964, p. 317.

6. E. Westermark, *Wit and Wisdom in Morocco*, p. 329. The first two proverbs can be traced to the second caliph, Umar Ibn al-Khattab. See al-Ghazali's *Revivification*, p. 44.

7. Koran, sura 4: 34. See remarks on the subject of beating in al-Ghazali, *Revivification*, p. 49; J. Schacht, *Introduction to Islamic Law*, p. 166; and Y. Linant de Bellefonds, *Traité de Droit musulman comparé*, The Hague and Paris 1965, p. 294.

8. Al-Bukhari, *al-Jami' al-Sahih*, p. 448, K: 67, B: 93; Tarmidi, *Sunan al-Tarmidi*, p. 415, B: 11, H: 1173.

9. Article 56, *Code du Status Personnel*.

10. *Dahshousha* is a symbolic nuptial tent made of drapes arranged within the nuptial room to emphasize the privacy of the married couple in the usually overcrowded house where the marriage takes place.

11. Al-Ghazali, *Revivification*, p. 56.

12. Koran, sura 4: 43.

13. Al-Ghazali, *Revivification*, p. 28.

14. Ibid., p. 50.

15. Ibid., p. 49.

16. Sandor Ferenczi, *Thalassa, A Theory of Genitality*, New York 1968, p. 17.

17. Al-Ghazali, *Revivification* p. 50. The verse is from the Koran, sura 25: 54. Other reports on the words a Muslim is supposed to pronounce during coitus are in Imam Bukhari, *al-Jami' al-Sahih*, p. 439, K: 67, B: 66; and Imam Tarmidi,

Sunan al-Tarmidi, p. 277, B: 8, H: 1098.

18. Max Weber, 'Religious Rejections of the World and Their Directions', in *From Max Weber*, translated by H. Gerth and C. Wright Mills, New York 1958, p. 347.

19. Koran, sura 2: 165.

20. Koran, sura 3: 4.

21. On God's jealousy, see Imam Bukhari, *al-Jami' al-Sahih*, p. 451, K: 67, B: 107, 106; and Imam Tarmidi, *Sunan al-Tarmidi*, p. 417, B: 14, H: 1178.

22. E. Westermark, *Wit and Wisdom*, p. 329.

23. W. Stephens, *The Oedipus Complex, Cross Cultural Evidence*, New York 1962, p. 6.

24. The master of a concubine can choose to limit her to a domestic function or to raise her to the status of lover with privileges, including the legitimacy of her children and their right to inherit.

25. The *hjar*: if a man is not attracted anymore by a concubine, he can refuse interaction with her, even at the verbal level, and her dismissal often reflects on the children's position within the harem community. The female object of *hjar* loses her status and her rights as favourite and lover and she is often looked down upon by her fellow wives and concubines. Often she is associated with 'bad luck' and the evil eye.

26. The rate in Morocco in 1952 was already very low—6.6%. It has probably decreased since then. See William Goode, *World Revolution and Family Patterns*, New York 1963, p. 103; also R. Patai, *Society, Culture and Change in the Middle East*, Philadelphia 1962, pp. 92–93.

27. Al-Ghazali, *Revivification*, p. 48.

28. Ibn Saad, *al-Tabaqat*, vol. 8, p. 192; see also al-Bukhari, *al-Jami' al-Sahih*, p. 412, K: 67, B: 4.

29. D. J. L. Roland, 'Développement de la Personnalité et Incidences de l'Environnement au Maroc', *Maroc Médical*, December 1964, pp. 269–272.

30. M. Achour, 'Vue particulière du Problème de l'Environnement en fonction du milieu scolaire marocain', *Maroc Médical*, December 1964, p. 329.

Chapter 7

1. The link between the child's experience with his mother and his capacity to relate to a person of the other sex is the crux of the Freudian concept of Oedipus complex.

2. P. Slater, *The Glory of Hera*, Boston 1968, p. 414.

3. Koran, sura 46: 15.

4. Koran, sura 4: 1, sura 31: 14, sura 6: 152, sura 17: 23, sura 29: 8.

5. Sigmund Freud, 'The Most Prevalent Form of Degradation of Erotic Life', in *Sexuality and the Psychology of Love*, New York 1970.

6. Dorothy Blisten, *The World of the Family*, New York 1963, pp. 204–205.

7. Sidi Abderahman al-Majdoub, in *Les Quatrains du Mejdoub le Sarcastique, Poète Maghrebin du XVIème siècle*, p. 180.

8. E. Westermark, *Wit and Wisdom*, p. 326.

9. Al-Majdoub, *Les Quatrains du Mejdoub*, p. 180.

10. P. Slater, *The Glory of Hera*, p. 30.

11. Article 36, *Code du Statut Personnel*. E. Goffman points out the tactical importance of deference rules in authoritarian relationships, in *Asylums*, New

190

York 1961, p. 115.
12. E. Goffman, *Asylums*, p. 41.

Chapter 8

1. The term 'territoriality', however, is really too primitive for the phenomenon, which is a sophisticated, manifold use of space. Hall's concept of 'proxemics' is more suitable:

> Proxemics is the term I have coined for the interrelated observations and theories of man's use of space and a specialized elaboration of culture. [Edward Hall, *The Hidden Dimension*, New York 1969, p. 1]

According to Hall, the dangers are great, given the sensuous dimension of any physical interaction, of involving the individuals in an atmosphere of ambiguous signs, unconsciously sent and received.

> Man's sense of space is closely related to his sense of self, which is in an intimate transaction with his environment. Man can be viewed as having visual, kinesthetic, tactile, and thermal aspects of his self which may be either inhibited or encouraged to develop by his environment. [*The Hidden Dimension*, p. 63.]

2. In *Purity and Danger*, Baltimore 1970, Mary Douglas emphasized the links in social structure between the concept of boundaries, the concept of danger, and the concept of power.

3. Ibid., p. 14.

4. In Moroccan folklore women are considered to be the repository of devilish forces: Edmund Doutte, *Magie et Religion dans l'Afrique du Nord*, Algiers 1908, p. 33; also, E. Westermark, *The Belief in Spirits in Morocco*, p. 22. The Moroccan psychologist Abelwanad Radi in 'Processus de socialisation de l'enfant marocain', *Etudes Philosophiques et Littéraires*, no. 4, April 1969, attributes to women the responsibility for introducing children to the world of the irrational, of spirits.

5. The term 'universe' is used here in the sense P. L. Berger and T. Luckman use it in *The Social Construction of Reality*, New York 1967.

6. Max Weber, *The Theory of Social and Economic Organization*, New York 1964, p. 136.

7. Ibid., p. 132.

8. To foster 'homosocial' relations does not necessarily mean to drive members of a society to practise what one Palestinian sociologist has called 'homosociality': the inclination to spend most of one's time, most of one's life, with individuals of the same sex. Homosociality entails fear of the other sex, and avoidance or limitation of controls with it. Obviously, homosociality is not peculiar to Arab society. Moreover, any institution or practice that tends to degrade the female body may be considered homosocial, and in this sense the advanced capitalist countries, with their pornography industry, would be prime examples.

9. More specifically, it condemned the practice of wearing wigs, which seems to have been quite common among Arab women in the seventh century

(al-Bukhari, *al-Jami' al-Sahih*, p. 447 K: 67). Tattooing, also condemned by Islam, is still practised in Morocco, and some of the tattoos have unequivocal erotic meanings. (J. Herber, 'Tatouage du Pubis au Maroc', *Revue d'Ethnie*, vol. 3, 1922.)

10. Koran, sura 24.

11. Al-Ghazali, *Revivification*, p. 35.

12. Ibid., p. 28.

13. Malika Belghiti, 'Les Relations Féminines et le Statut de la Femme dans la Famille Rurale', *Collection du Bulletin Economique et Social du Maroc*, Rabat 1970, p. 57.

14. The French anthropologist Germaine Tillion (*The Republic of Cousins*, Al Saqi Books, London 1983) noted that peasant women newly arrived to towns usually adopt the practice of veiling. She found it strange that women who were not veiled before adopted the veil willingly. I think that this phenomenon could be very easily interpreted if one remembers that for the rural woman who has recently emigrated to the town, the veil is a sign of upward mobility—the expression of her newly acquired status as urbanite.

15. M. Belghiti, 'Les Relations Féminines', p. 58.

16. Women are especially restricted when in a space they should have a right to: the mosque. In Morocco they may use only a specified area, usually a narrow, marginal, dark corner behind the male space. Although the Prophet allowed women to go to mosques, their right to be there was, during Islam's fourteen centuries of existence, frequently in doubt and is often still subject to the husband's authorization. (Al-Bukhari, *al-Jami' al-Sahih*, p. 453, K: 67, B: 115.)

17. P. Pascon and M. Bentahar, '269 Jeunes Ruraux', p. 63.

18. My own experience has been that women are more or less harassed depending on the socio-economic features of the place they are walking. Harassment is more systematic in small and medium-sized than in large cities. It is more intense in the poor neighbourhoods and slums of Rabat and Casablanca than in the middle-class areas of these same cities. It also varies according to the legitimacy of the reason you are on the street: harassment is less intense at a post-office queue than it would be if you succumb to the desire to have an ice cream or some chips in a café in a poor neighbourhood. Of course, there are some situations that concern only minorities. In those cases the mechanisms are more difficult to grasp, such as, for instance, the harassment of women who drive cars, which seems to be governed by a completely different system of references. Your chances of being harassed seem to be greater if you drive an old small car than if you are in a big gleaming machine.

19. E. Hall, *The Hidden Dimension*, p. 156.

20. Ibid., p. 163.

21. Erving Goffman, *Behaviour in Public Places*, New York 1966, p. 143.

22. Frantz Fanon, *A Dying Colonialism*, New York 1967, p. 53. It is interesting to note that Fanon thought the incidents were 'funny'. For a man with Fanon's sensitivity to segregation and preoccupation with revolutionary assertion of human rights, his remark is puzzling to say the least.

23. Personal communication to the author.

24. Chérifa Alaoui el-Mdaghri, 'Le Travail féminin: cas de la Fonction publique au Maroc en 1980', Ecole Nationale d'Administration Publique, Rabat, cycle supérieur, no. 11, promotion 1980–81.

Chapter 9

1. On the situation of the labour market, see A. Agouram and A. Belal, 'Bilan de l'Economie Marocaine depuis l'Independence', *BESM*, XXXII, p. 116. According to the authors, unemployment in urban centres reaches 30% to 50% and hits 60% in rural areas. They emphasize the impact of this situation on the future by showing that while the number of labourers increases each year at a rate of 3%, the number of jobs increases at a rate of only 2%.

2. *Code du Statut Personnel*, Dahir no. 1-57-343, in *Bulletin Officiel* no. 2354, 6 December 1957.

3. Emile Durkheim, 'L'Education Morale', in *Selected Writings*, edited by A. Giddens, Cambridge 1972, p. 174.

4. Mao Tse-Tung, in Bruce Shaw's abridged version of Peking's authorized edition of *Selected Works of Mao Tse-Tung*, New York 1970.

5. A decision to abolish pre-existing privileges, mainly those based on sexual differences, is a very daring decision on the part of any regime, and more so on the part of a new regime. It is a very unpopular step indeed. The Chinese Communist regime had to face and deal with the resistance the male Chinese population posed to such measures. See C. K. Yang, *Chinese Communist Society: The Family and the Village*, Cambridge, Mass. 1965, particularly Part I, 'The Chinese Family in the Communist Revolution'.

6. *1950 Marrriage Law of the People's Republic of China*, Article 9.

7. *Code du Statut Personnel*, Article 35.

8. Personal communication from *qadis* and lawyers, supplemented by observation in Rabat's Sadad court during February 1974.

9. A brief sketch of the history of the education systems promoted by the French protectorate in Morocco is in John Halstead's *Rebirth of a Nation: The Origin and Rise of Moroccan Nationalism 1912–1944*, Cambridge, Mass. 1969, pp. 98–114.

10. André Révérand, *Un Lyautey inconnu*, Paris 1980.

11. Fatima Hassar, 'The Special Problems of Young Women and Mothers with Regard to Their Families and Professional Careers', read at the International Conference of Parents Associations, 22–28 July 1962. Published by the Ministry of Education, Rabat.

12. Allal al-Fasi, *The Independence Movements in Arab North Africa*, p. 413.

13. Fatima Hassar, 'Special Problems of Young Women', p. 86.

14. *Le Maroc en Chiffres*, 2nd ed., Rabat 1971, p. 25.

15. Muhammad Lahbabi, *Les Années 80 de notre Jeunesse*, Casablanca 1970, p. 55.

16. *Le Maroc en Chiffres*, p. 25.

17. An ever-rising number of young researchers are choosing to work on the impact of female access to education and jobs and on family relations, in particular a group of about thirty people calling themselves the 'Groupe de Recherche Scientifique sur la Femme, la Famille, et l'Enfant au Maroc', located at the law school in Rabat.

18. Fatima Mernissi, 'Historical Insights for New Population Strategies: Women in Precolonial Morocco', UNESCO, Paris 1978; also Mernissi, 'Développement capitaliste et perceptions des femmes dans la société musulmane: les paysannes du Gharb', International Labour Office, WEP 10-4-04-90, Geneva, May 1981.

19. Moroccan economists and statisticians, like their European and Latin American colleagues, generally classified most rural women, who work fourteen hours a day, as 'women at home' and therefore inactive. Happily, many Moroccan economists and statisticians are young and open-minded; they are now reviewing their categories of labour in general, and of female labour in particular. See Cherkaoui Abdelinalek's book on 'social indicators' (Casablanca 1981), especially chapter 3, on 'inquiry into urban employment' conducted in 1976.

20. All data in this section is taken from volume II of the *Recensement Général de la Population et de l'Habitat*, 1971, unless otherwise noted.

21. Ibid., p. 12.

22. 'Enquête sur l'emploi urbain', Rabat Bureau of Statistics, 1976, p. 13.

23. *Recensement Général de la Population*, 1971, vol. 2, p. 6.

24. Wilhelm Reich, *The Mass Psychology of Fascism*, New York 1970, p. 60.

25. Ibid., p. 31.

26. Ibid., p. 55.

27. See *Honour and Shame, the Values of Mediterranean Society*, edited by J. G. Peristiany, Chicago 1966. Peristiany's introduction is a concise description of the psycho-social mechanisms operating under the concept of honour. One feature of these mechanisms is that the men in such societies do not have a source of self-esteem within themselves but only attached to subjects outside themselves.

28. The political, professional, and economic frustrations of men are often the object of inhibitions, of more or less conscious censor mechanisms. The case of a young (thirty-year-old) employee at the planning ministry is unfortunately fairly typical: he had serious problems gaining promotion and threatened his wife, a medical doctor, with divorce because she 'will not obey me'. Even the *qadis* (judges), who are used to conjugal conflicts, were surprised by this paradoxical instance of a young husband who had married an 'employed woman' trying to make her obey. 'I don't understand', said a young *qadi* of the Rabat court, 'why men who choose to marry a woman who works and gets a salary just like them insist on the obedience that is due them.'

29. J. Whiting and I. Child, *Child Training and Personality*, New Haven 1953, p. 276.

30. W. Reich, *Mass Psychology of Fascism*, p. 32.

31. In interviews with young female employees from the urban middle class conducted between 1975 and 1980, I found many who reported that when the couple visited the husband's family, the husband, out of 'respect', insisted that his wife share his mother's bed. Many Moroccan men carry around photographs of their mothers in their wallets and monotonously and repeatedly inform the women they are seeing with 'serious intentions' that mother is the woman they love most in the world. During the summer of 1982 a thirty-year-old woman lawyer in Casablanca received a marriage proposal from a charming 34-year-old colleague of hers. When she asked him, 'Why me?', he replied ardently: 'I chose you from the first day I saw you in court, because you look so much like my mother. You're a carbon copy—same eyes, same size, . . .' The young woman politely declined his offer and he never understood why he had been rejected. Many of the divorces that come before Moroccan courts are brought on by the mother-in-law. A systematic study of the phenomenon would be interesting.

32. *Ana qarran daba* ('Now I'm a cuckold') is a formula pronounced by an

annoyed husband whose wife is not home at the usual time.

Conclusion

1. Mariarosa Della Costa, *Women and the Subversion of the Community*, Bristol 1972.

2. 'Communism in Marriage', article by David Riazanov, published in Moscow in 1926, reproduced in *al-Mar'a wa al-Ishtiraqiya* (Women and Socialism), translated and edited by George Tarabishi, Beirut 1974 (second edition), pp. 33–70.

3. Dr. Salwa Khammash, *al-Mar'a al-Arabiya wa'l-Mujtama al-Taqlidiya* (Arab Women and Traditional Society), Beirut 1973, particularly chapter V (the relation between the sexes) and chaper VII (the position of the wife).

4. George Tarabishi, in his introduction to *Women and Socialism*, p. 13.

5. The article states: 'Killing, wounding, and beating are excusable if they are committed by a husband against his wife and/or her accomplice at the moment that he surprises them *in flagrante delicto* committing adultery.'

6. Philip Slater, *The Glory of Hera*, p. 73.

7. Al-Majdoub, p. 144.

8. Dr. Sadiq Jalal al-Azm, *Fi'l-Hubb wa'l-Hubb al-Udri* (On Love and Udrite Love), second edition, Beirut 1974, pp. 92 ff.

9. Ibid.

10. Tahar Labib Djedidi, 'La Poésie Amoureuse des Arabes', Algiers 1974.

11. Ibid., pp. 76, 134, 140, 142.

12. Sadiq al-Azm, pp. 110–111.

13. Ibid., p. 28.

14. Abdallah Laroui, 'La Crise des Intellectuels Arabes', paper read at colloquium in Louvain, 1970, published in *La Crise des Intellectuels Arabes*, Paris 1974.

15. George Tarabishi, introduction to Women and Socialism, p. 13.

Index

Abbott, Nabia 184
Abdelinalek, Cherkaoui 193
Abdel-Malek, Anouar 16, 180
Achour, M. 189
al-Afghani, Said 179
Afifi, A. 179
Agouram, Abdeljalil 187, 192
Aisha (wife of the Prophet) 53, 55–58, 75, 117, 184
Aisha, Princess (daughter of Muhammad V, King of Morocco) 155
Alaoui, Qadi Moulay Mustapha, Professor 93, 98, 118, 127
al-Albani, Muhammad Nasr al-Din 179
al-'Ali, Salah Ahmad 66, 185
Allah 8, 17–19, 44–45, 50–51, 57, 59, 63, 81, 82, 106, 108, 112, 113, 115, 138, 144, 164, 184
Amina (great-granddaughter of the Prophet) 70–71
Amin, Qasim 13–14, 31, 180, 182, 187
Amin, Samir 83, 181, 187
Amr, Dubaa Bint 56
Amr, Salama Bint 69
al-Aqqad, Abbas Mahmud 32–33, 38, 57, 179, 182
Arab League 17
aruba 108
aryana 144
'azl 37
al-Azm, Sadiq Jalal 174, 176, 194

ba'al 73–75
baghaya 76
Bakr, Abu 71–72, 187
Beeston, A. F. L. 73, 186
Belal, A. 181, 187, 192
Belghiti, Malika 101, 142, 188, 191
de Bellefonds, Y. Linant 188
Bentahar, M. 143, 187, 188, 191
Berger, P. L. 190
Blisten, Dorothy 189
Briffault, R. 187
Bukhari, Imam 59, 65, 66, 75–77, 183–86, 188, 189, 191

Cantwell-Smith, Wilfred 180
Cheikh, T. Ben 181
Child, I. 193
Coatalen, Paul 180
Code du Statut Personnel 11, 24, 46, 57, 59, 60, 61–64, 109–10, 148, 152, 163, 171, 179, 185, 188, 189, 192

al-Dahhak, Fatima Bint 52
Della Costa, Mariarosa 165, 194
Djedidi, Tahar Labib 174, 194
Douglas, Mary 190
Doutte, Edmund 190
Durkheim, Emile 150, 192

Fanon, Frantz 191
Fares, Edouard 187
al-Fasi, Allal 16–17, 155, 180, 192

Fatima (daughter of the
    Prophet) 70–71, 187
Ferenczi, Sandor 188
fitna 31, 39, 41–42, 44, 53–54, 82,
    113
Forde, Daryll 187
Fox, Robin 187
Freud, Sigmund 27, 32–41, 44,
    182, 183, 189

Gerth, H. 189
al-Ghazali, Abu Hamid (see
    Imam Ghazali)
Gibb, H. A. R. 20, 180, 181
Giddens, A. 192
Glubb, Sir John 186
Goffman, Erving 130, 189, 190,
    191
Goldziher, Ignaz 183
Goode, William 189
guellassa 123

Hafsa (wife of the Prophet) 55
al-Hajawi, Muhammad
    al-Mahdi 179, 187
Hall, Edward 143, 190, 191
Halstead, John 192
hammam 123, 131, 143, 161
Hanbal, Abu 181
Hanifa, Abu 181
al-Harith, Juwariya Bint 56
Hashim (great-grandfather of
    the Prophet) 68–69
Hassar, Fatima 192
Herber, J. 191
hiba 52
hijra 46, 81
hjar 116, 189
hma 122, 127, 130, 131
htewta 162
al-Hussein, Sakina Bint 186
Huyay, Safiya Bint 54–55

Ibn Abd al-Muttalib, Abdallah
    69
Ibn Abi Talib, Ali 70

Ibn Abi Umayyah, al-Muhajir 72
Ibn Ali, Hasan (grandson of the
    Prophet) 50
Ibn Anas, Malik (see Iman
    Malik)
Ibn Bashir, Muhammad 75
Ibn Habib al-Baghdadi 65, 69,
    71, 72, 185, 186
Ibn Hisham 69, 115, 183, 186
Ibn Ishaq 186
Ibn Khaldun 180, 182
Ibn al-Khali 115
Ibn Murad, Sheikh 15
Ibn Saad 66, 67, 68, 182, 184, 185,
    186, 189
Ibn Shihab 75
Ibn Umar, Zaid 71
Ibn al-Zubair, Urwah 75
Ibrahim (son of the Prophet) 51,
    55
idda 62–64, 67, 81, 185
ila 60
Imam Ghazali 28, 32–40, 44, 45,
    47, 60, 89, 108, 110, 112–13,
    141, 182, 183, 184, 185, 188,
    189, 191
Imam Malik 11, 24, 61–64, 139,
    180, 181, 184, 185
Imam Muslim 42, 183
al-Isfahani, Abu-al-Faraj 186

jahiliya 46, 61, 65, 75, 76, 84–85,
    166
Jahsh, Zainab Bint 56–57

Ka'ab, Mulaika Bint 52–53
Kandisha, Aisha 42
karha 111–112
Khammash, Salwa 194
al-Khatim, Leila Bint 51–52, 70
Khelifa, B. 183
khul' 61–62
Khuwalid, Khadija Bint 51
Koran, the 32, 33, 46–50, 57,
    63–64, 80, 81, 111, 113, 179,
    181, 183, 184, 185, 186, 188,

189, 191

Lahbabi, Muhammad 192
Lalla 129
Laroui, Abdallah 23, 180, 181, 194
Lerner, Daniel 15–16, 180
Linton, Ralph 34, 182
Luckman, T. 190
Lyautey, General 153–54

ma' 37
al-Maghribi, Abd al-Qadir 179
al-Majdoub, Sidi Abderahman 43, 183, 189, 194
Malekite school 24, 63, 181
Malinowski, B. 187
Maria, the Copt (wife of the Prophet) 51, 55
al-Mawdudi, Abu'l-Ala 179
el-Mdaghri, Chérifa Alaoui 191
Mernissi, Fatima 192
Mills, C. Wright 189
Muhammad (the Prophet) 17–18, 21, 22, 27–28, 30, 37, 40–43, 51–60, 64, 67, 69–70, 71, 72, 76, 79, 80, 82, 108, 110–11, 117, 142, 184, 185, 186
Muhammad V (king of Morocco) 155
muhsan 58
al-Munajid, Salah al-Din 183
Murdock, George 30, 182
Musa, Salama 13, 78, 180, 181, 187
Muslim, Abu al-Hasan (see Imam Muslim)
mut'a 66, 77–78
al-Muttalib, Abd (grandfather of the Prophet) 68–69

Naja, Mustafa 179
al-Naqdi, Jafar 179
al-Numan, Asma Bint 52–53

d'Ormesson, Wladimir 153

Pascon, P. 143, 187, 188, 191
Patai, R. 189
Peristiany, J. G. 193
Pickthall, Mohammed Marmaduke 179, 187
Prophet, the (see Muhammad the Prophet)

qaid 33
al-Qaramani, Abd al-Qadir 179
al-Qumaili, Sadiq 179

Radcliffe-Brown, A. R. 187
Radi, Abelwanad 190
Ramadan 143
Reich, Wilhelm 160, 163, 193
Révérand, André 153, 192
Riazanov, David 194
Roland, D. J. L. 189
Rosenthal, Franz 180, 182

sadiqa 73–75
al-Salah, Murad 180
al-Sanusi, Abu Radwan 179
Scelles-Millie, J. 183
Schacht, Joseph 22, 180, 181, 185, 188
Schultz, A. 182
al-Shafi'i, Abu Abdullah Muhammad 181
Shaltut, Mahmud, 179
shari'a 12, 14, 18, 21–23, 135, 154, 163
Sharik, Umm 51
Shaw, Bruce 192
al-Shayyal, Muhammad 179
Shia 77
sidi 162
Slater, Philip 121, 170, 189, 194
Smith, Robertson 73–74, 78, 186, 187
Stannard, Una 182
Stephens, W. 189
Stern, Gertrude 67–68, 180, 185, 186

tamlik 61–62
Tarabishi, George 169, 176, 194
al-Tarmidi, Abu Issa 183, 184,
    185, 186, 188, 189
teyyaba 123
Tillion, Germaine 191

Umar, Caliph 59, 187, 188
umma 17–23, 48, 78, 80, 82, 105,
    138–39, 142, 146, 169, 184
Utba, Hind Bint 184–85
Uthman, Caliph 187

Vesey-Fitzgerald, S. G. 181

Wahb, Amina Bint 69–70
Watt, Montgomery 79–80, 82,
    180, 185, 186, 187
Weber, Max 146, 189, 190
Westermark, Edward 183, 188,
    189, 190
Whiting, J. 193

Yang, C. K. 192

Zaid (adopted son of the
    Prophet) 56–57
Zaid, Atika Bint 59
Zayd, Rayhana Bint 55, 70
Zaynab (wife of the Prophet) 42
Zedong, Mao 151, 192
zina 49, 54, 58–60, 64, 74, 80, 81,
    102, 144, 184–85